CW00495302

Making
Soft Dolls

Steffi Stern

Let's Sew Some Love!

Hawthorn Press

Making Soft Dolls © 2020 Steffi Stern

Steffi Stern is hereby identified as the author of this work in accordance with section 77 of the Copyright, Designs and Patent Act, 1988. She asserts and gives notice of her moral right under this Act.

Hawthorn Press

Published by Hawthorn Press, Hawthorn House,
1 Lansdown Lane, Stroud, Gloucestershire, GL5 1BJ, UK
Tel: (01453) 757040
Email: info@hawthornpress.com
Website: www.hawthornpress.com

All rights reserved. No part of this book may be reproduced, stored in a retrieval system or transmitted in any form by any means (electronic or mechanical, through reprography, digital transmission, recording or otherwise) without prior written permission of the publisher.

Extract from *Flour Babies* © Anne Fine, published with permission from Penguin Books and David Higham.

Photographs © Oliver Perrott
Additional photography by Steffi Stern
Illustrations and design by Lucy Guenot
Typeset in 'The Sans' and 'Maiandra' fonts
Front cover photography © Sylvain Guenot

Printed in UK by Short Run Press Ltd, Exeter
Printed on environmentally friendly paper manufactured from renewable forest stock and other controlled sources.

Every effort has been made to trace the ownership of all copyrighted material. If any omission has been made, please bring this to the publisher's attention so that proper acknowledgement may be given in future editions. The views expressed in this book are not necessarily those of the publisher.

British Library Cataloguing in Publication Data applied for

ISBN 978-1-912480-05-0

Making Soft Dolls

Steffi Stern

Simple Waldorf designs to sew and love

Hawthorn Press

Dedication

This book is dedicated to my late mother, Mutti whose hands I have never seen without knitting needles or a crochet hook and who has taught me to use my hands to their best ability, keep my mind open that anything is possible and most of all the importance of not taking yourself too seriously!

Contents

Foreword

What is a Waldorf Doll?

Waldorf, or soft, dolls are much loved with children keeping them long into adulthood, often to be handed down to children or grandchildren, along with their story. But what explains our love for and attachment to such dolls? A Waldorf doll has some disadvantages for current tastes: it can't be bought, it is modest looking and not always beautiful, one has to make it oneself, it is never simply available and may look somewhat unfinished compared with a Barbie doll.

Waldorf dolls can be bought in Waldorf schools, in some toy stores, and of course on the internet. There are even a number of manufacturers that have applied for 'Waldorf doll' patents. But are these commercially available dolls actually the real, original Waldorf doll? In this comprehensive book, *Making Soft Dolls*, Steffi guides us through the process of making our own dolls for ourselves, for our children or for our grandchildren. The point is to make it yourself and imbue it with love that you can pass on.

Rudolf Steiner often spoke about the special qualities and needs of the young child, as well as the inner attitude and soul qualities that the adult needs to acquire in order to support the development of the child. However, if one is looking for a detailed description of what a Waldorf kindergarten should look like and the concrete activities that should take place there, these are not to be found in Steiner's work. No programme and no recipes!

There are, however, a few exceptions that Steiner described quite concretely and the doll is one of these. In his first book on education Steiner described what the original Waldorf doll could look like:

'You can make a doll for a child by folding up an old napkin, twisting two corners into legs, the other two corners into arms, a knot for the head, and painting eyes, nose and mouth with blots of ink.'

An old 'doll' napkin will look different each time and thus the Waldorf doll will look completely different each time, and can adapt to the context of each family, the capacities of the educator and the desire and imagination of the children. It is flexible, open and multicultural – very modern!

Steiner was keen on promoting these lively doll companions and explains why they are so important for the development of the child. 'With the so-called beautiful doll we hinder the child from developing the unfolding of a wonderfully delicate, awakening imagination.'

The French psychologist Régine Démarthes once said, *'It is the way a child plays with a toy that makes it alive in the child's eyes. But when the toy imposes its complexity on the child, it cripples the child's creative imagination.'*

'Closed' toys determine the course and the outcome of play, while toys that are open-ended leave the child free to independently shape the course of play, fostering creativity and the capacity for problem-solving. The simple cloth doll relies on the child's creativity. It is open-ended and complete only through activity, so those delicate imaginations can develop freely.

Philipp Reubke is a senior Waldorf kindergarten teacher and member of the International Association of Waldorf Kindergartens (IASWECE)

Introduction

I have crafted and created throughout my whole childhood and continue to do so to this day. The projects in this book are easy and accessible for everybody. I am not a dressmaker and only sew by hand. I love knitting and crocheting but complicated patterns leave me confused. The purpose of this book is to introduce you to doll-making and to help those who already make dolls to try other methods and ideas. The dolls in this book are relatively simple projects that enable you to create something beautiful, practical and tactile; something of good enough quality to be used every day. The process of making the doll can be as important, if not more important, than the finished project. I sincerely hope that any doll you make from this book will be loved, squeezed, and played with, tucked into bed or into a pocket to keep safe, cuddled and kissed! Perhaps they will look worn and torn and have dirty faces and in years to come, maybe they will need mending, or maybe they will look perfect forever! So long as the doll has filled a space in someone's heart, the purpose of the making and the doll itself has been fulfilled.

I made my first doll 15 years ago. I will never forget the total empowerment I felt of being able to make a toy, not just a toy but a doll for my baby who was not even one year old. The doll itself was such a simple one, just a soft head with a little hair, a sewn-on hat and a triangular body stuffed very loosely with carded sheep wool. The sense of pride it gave me is hard to put into words. It was a feeling of freedom and liberation that I was able to give to my children a tiny bit of myself forever captured in the shape of a toy that would be by their side. It was as if my love was there with them, even when I was not. There's a difference between buying a toy from a shop shelf, perhaps a mass-produced product, and the love you feel when you make something yourself. I remember the feeling of passionately filling every stitch with my love and hope and feeding that into that first doll.

My wish is for everybody to experience that feeling of warmth and satisfaction when sewing a little love into a handmade doll, whatever the reason you are making it.

My hope is that you as the reader of this book will find the confidence and motivation to make your very own soft doll, with the results perhaps beyond what you imagined.

Steffi Stern

Why Waldorf Dolls?

If you are not familiar with a Waldorf doll it might be useful to explain first of all what defines these dolls. Wikipedia online has this as its interpretation:

A Waldorf doll (also called Steiner doll) is a form of doll compatible with Waldorf (or Steiner) education philosophies. Made of natural materials, such as fine woollen or cotton skin-toned fabric, generally filled with pure wool stuffing; hair and clothing materials are also made from natural fibres. The doll makers use techniques which draw on traditional European doll-making. The doll's appearance is intentionally simple in order to allow the child playing with it to develop the imagination and creative play. For instance, it has either no features, or a simple neutral expression. The legs and arms are soft and if flexible allow natural postures. They are ideally entirely natural.

This does not mean that a Waldorf doll is only suitable for people who educate their children the Waldorf way. If you are a lover of natural materials, handmade toys, and keeping features simple and innocent, then this is a great way to create dolls for people old and young, including yourself!

If there was a spectrum of dolls where one end represents 'handmade, timeless, classic and unique' and the other 'contemporary, cartoonish, mass produced', Waldorf dolls would be at the timeless and classic end. In our modern world we find plenty of assembly line-produced dolls, often with exaggerated features (huge eyes, highlighted mouths, hard bodies made from plastic, hair from man-made fibre) – all made to look the same. The handmade Waldorf doll fits into another space in a child's or adult's life: something to cuddle, to keep as an heirloom, to appreciate through the years, to know that only one of its kind exists into which one can pour love. A doll that means so many different things to so many different people: a brother, a sister, a lost child, a lost childhood, fond memories, a baby to nurture, a child to care for, a comforter, a friend and companion.

The beauty of handmade Waldorf dolls is that the meaning of the dolls starts as soon as you gather the materials to create one! The journey starts with the making, the care and thought that is put into it, the personalisation, the materials you choose, the reasons why you are making it and how you feel whilst creating one. These reasons can be so manifold and can even change in the process. The fate of the doll may change too: you may decide to keep it when it was meant to be a gift or you may make it a gift when you had not planned to give it away.

Maybe you decide to make a doll for a baby or child (your own or someone else's). Perhaps the doll is for you and you take great pleasure in designing it to sit on your sofa for you to admire. Another reason could be that you are making it for a friend or family member who is in need of such a gift, perhaps a person at the end of their life or somebody who suffers from dementia? Perhaps the doll is made to heal yourself or somebody else. Maybe you are helping another person (child or adult) to make a doll.

I used to ask my children what colour hair and eyes they would like on their dolls, whether it should be a boy or girl. The making of the doll can be as powerful as the handmade doll itself. It is important to take a moment and be aware of why the doll is being made; with every stitch a little of that significance is added.

The meaning of a handmade doll changes over the years. I have found that a handmade doll has many stages in its life as the years go by. It may be that they get more appreciated as the years pass (by children growing older or adults going through different stages in their lives). They may get passed on and become meaningful in other ways. I treasure the doll 'Peter Püppi' that my grandmother originally made for my father: it was a loved toy for my cousins and me and then for my children and who knows what may be in store for Peter in the future? Little did my grandmother know that her 'after the war' doll, made with the few materials that she could find, would become such a treasured heirloom.

Doll Stories

When I started making dolls I found that many doll-making patterns were quite challenging and confusing, especially as you had to make all the body parts separately and then sew them together. I was so intimidated by the details in these patterns that I designed my own 'all-in-one' doll. As I shared my template with people, I was privileged to hear their 'doll stories' and I began to realise that making dolls holds a special place in people's lives and for far more profound reasons than I ever imagined.

I remember Sandy, a mother of six, a grandmother and even great-grandmother who, sadly had lost her only son when he was small. Making a doll brought her a little comfort. She talked to the dolls she made and they became little people with characters – I loved seeing how they evolved. She told me once that she had made a little doll for her own mother, who was then in a dementia care home, and how her mother loved holding the soft doll and squeezing it. She ended up making a whole load of dolls for other people in the home. She also told me that she had made a little doll for her grandson who was bullied at school, to keep in his pocket so he could feel loved when he was frightened and worried. She sewed a heart or special symbol into the body of each doll, which I found very charming and thoughtful.

On another occasion I had a lady visit me who was making dolls with women in prison who had lost a baby. The dolls were simple – a small pouch doll that would fit into a pocket – and they always had something glittery or glitzy on them. It made them extra special for these women, a real treasure they could hide away and keep safe when they weren't able to do this with their real babies.

Another woman uses doll-making as a therapeutic process with young women who suffer from anorexia. What better way to experience making a body so totally free of shape while also soft and comforting?

Once I made a doll for one of my children and they rejected her. I was heartbroken and it took me a while to learn that sometimes it is not love at first sight but it might take a little longer to grow. Now that my children are growing up, the handmade dolls have grown in value and esteem and they all remember that these were a very special gift. They are kept safe and have become heirlooms.

I believe that boys need dolls to play with too and remember one story about my own family. My three girls were playing very sweetly with their babies and it was all about nurturing, caring and organising the daily routines to keep their babies fed, warm, clean and amused. My son joined in their game with his doll and instantly he announced that there was an emergency. A fire had broken out in the house and he was the fireman who promptly initiated that the 'babies' were to be lowered from the window on the first floor via a rope into the garden, where he then transported them very carefully on his digger shovel (aka ambulance) to hospital. The whole dynamic of the play shifted from peaceful to action adventure, but all parties concerned seemed happy to join in and play their roles.

Though I was rarely allowed to mention it to my son, he always had his dolls tucked up in bed beside him when it came to bedtime, even at an age when he would have been positively upset with me if I had ever told anybody! He loved his dolls in his quiet heroic way and I would not have wanted him to have missed out on this. The girls, on the other hand, were far more expressive about their love for their babies.

In her book *Flour Babies*, Anne Fine gives us an insight (albeit fictional, but it could be real) into a child's mind and why they might find an ally in a doll.

'I'll tell you what I like about you,' he said, staring into her big round eyes. 'You're very easy to get on with. You're not like Mum, always telling me to put my plate in the sink, or shut doors more quietly, or pick my shoes off the floor. You're not like Gran, always telling me how much I've grown, and asking what I'm going to do when I leave school. You don't want me different, like all my teachers do. You don't tease me, like Sue. And you don't run off and leave, like my Dad.'

You never know what deeper meaning a doll may have to somebody.

Reflecting on the many stories I have been told and the reasons why people engage in doll-making, I have come to believe that dolls are for everyone, not just for children. The making of the doll is often as important, if not sometimes more so, than the finished doll and all of us can benefit from a first, and a last, doll to complete the circle of life.

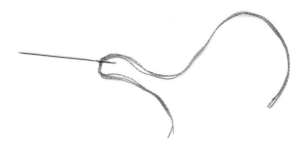

What You Need: Materials and Skills

Materials

You can source a lot of materials using things you already have and upcycling old garments; however there are some things that it would be a shame to compromise on and that includes the fabric for the skin for heads and bodies. The jersey I use has a natural colour and stretchy texture while being super strong.

Fabrics

STOCKINETTE

The skin-coloured jersey fabric I use is a specialist fabric, a soft knitted stretchy jersey also called stockinette or tricot fabric. What's so special about the doll-making stockinette is that it is made from 100 per cent cotton and comes in different shades of skin colour. This fabric is produced for the medical industry and is used for prosthetic limb bandaging. It is relatively difficult to source in the UK, especially the heavier (double knit) quality.

In this book I use two types of knit:

1. A single knit, double-sided stockinette that is reversible and slightly stretchy. It is best used for small dolls such as the dolls' house dolls and for heads because of its slightly smoother finish.

2. A double knit, single-sided stockinette that has a right and a wrong side. The right side looks like stocking stitch, the wrong side like purl stitch. While this fabric is still stretchy, it is thicker and less elastic than the single knit stockinette and used mostly for larger dolls.

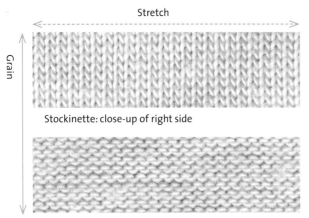

Stretch

Grain

Stockinette: close-up of right side

Stockinette: close-up of wrong side

The main thing to remember for both types of stockinette is that the grain always needs to run lengthways on the head and body, which means the stretch occurs sideways, to the left and right.

It is possible to use other jersey or stretchy cotton fabrics, but inevitably their stretchiness will vary and it may be challenging to find natural skin colours.

COTTON TUBE GAUZE, DIFFERENT SIZES

When making double-layered heads, especially when an eye line is being tied, I use cotton tube gauze, which is produced for the medical industry. The two sizes I use in this book are 1.5cm ($9/16$in) and 3.5cm ($13/8$in). The tubular shape is thin and strong enough to contain the stuffing well. It is possible to use an old lightweight cotton T-shirt of a light or neutral colour to make your own custom tubes.

VELOUR – OR NICKI FABRIC

This soft fabric is not dissimilar to velvet but is also stretchy. Ideally the velour used on dolls should be at least eighty per cent cotton, which again can be hard to source.

FLANNELETTE

This is also referred to as brushed cotton and is a soft fabric with little stretch. It works well for the simple triangle doll style but less so for any other designs as it does not stretch. You may have some old winter bed sheets that you can repurpose.

FELT

I use a wool-viscose mix felt, an easy felt to work with, and thin enough to be flexible for the small dolls' house dolls. 100 per cent wool felt can be more expensive and often too thick to use for tiny dolls. Acrylic or synthetic felt is often very soft, does not stay in shape and can be prone to tearing when sewing close to the edge. The wool-viscose felt is easy to sew and holds stitches well.

Stockinette single-sided

Cotton tube gauze narrow

Cotton tube gauze wide

Cotton flannelette

Felt

Felt in assorted colours

Tape measure

Velour – or Nicki fabric

Stockinette double-sided

Threads, wool and extras

WOOL BATTS FOR STUFFING

The wool batts for stuffing are a natural off-white or cream colour and feel very soft and bouncy. These work well for all the dolls, whether you stuff them really tightly, or keep them soft and squishy. The way it has been brushed (into a batt) means that it is a continuous sheet of wool (a little like batting) and therefore does not get lumpy. It can be torn off in a long strip, which works well to form a solid ball shape for a head, as you can wind it up on itself easily and tightly.

WOOL BATTS FOR THE NEEDLE FELTED HEADS

The best wool for making quick shapes and wrapping the pipe cleaners for the dolls' house dolls is a lanolin-rich wool batt. I favour an organic South German Merino, which is cold-washed to retain as much of the natural sheep fat as possible while still cleaning the wool. It is lovely to work with and as an added side benefit, leaves your hands feeling soft. It also means that it is slightly 'sticky' in a good way in that it wants to adhere to itself and needs less felting down with the felting needle.

THREADS FOR SEWING, EMBROIDERY AND TYING

There are three types of thread that you will use in this book.

1. Thread for sewing the bodies and heads. These should be strong sewing threads and whilst cotton is a natural choice, polyester threads are stronger and longer lasting. The dolls are likely to be handled a lot and need to endure being pulled and dragged.

2. Embroidery thread or floss is multi-stranded and is great for embroidering facial details. The strands can be separated for fine detailed work. This thread can also be used to sew together the dolls' house dolls' clothes and a contrasting colour looks good in a blanket stitch as an edging.

3. Thread for tying heads, hands and feet needs to be extra-strong and you can test it by trying to break it with your hands. Once you have the thread tight around the head to make an eye line and pull as hard as you can, you will be grateful for a non-breaking

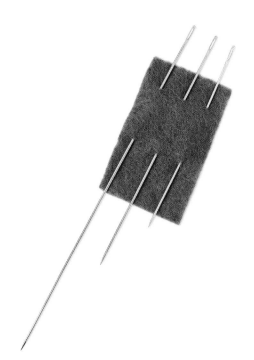

thread. I use a polyester thread specially designed for doll-making, though it has the appearance of a cotton thread. You can also use an extra-strong linen or button thread.

KNITTING YARN

I am a great lover of natural fibres, especially wool, and only use wool (or cotton) for the knitting and crochet projects in this book. Whatever you use, be mindful that you are quite possibly making a toy or something somebody will hold and cuddle, so the yarn should be soft. Merino and Blue Faced Leicester yarns and Alpaca are ideal.

TINY CARD EMBELLISHMENTS, RIBBONS, BUTTONS, LACE AND TRIMMINGS

I love tiny decorations such as flowers, satin bows, tiny buttons, stars, etc. I have a collection of these little decorations that have fallen off other toys or have been sold as card-making supplies. They provide such a wonderful opportunity to dress up your dolls' house dolls. You can sew them onto their clothes to make pockets or other features, braces, hair decorations, bow ties; even a large satin flower could become a fascinator. However, be aware that they can become a choking hazard for small children and babies.

Tiny buttons

Small embellishments

Extra-thin ribbon

Extra-strong
pipe cleaners

Felting wool

Wooden feet

Extra-strong linen thread

Skin-toned threads for sewing

Embroidery threads

Knitting wool

Mohair

Bouclé

Wool top

Mohair

Merino tops

Dyed sheep locks

Natural sheep locks

Bouclé

Wool batts

Wool nepps – for stuffing

Bouclé

Hair

There are no limits to what you may find suitable to use for hair, especially on tiny dolls. Whenever I see a scrap of wool or yarn I always wonder whether it would work for hair on a doll. My favourite materials are:

BOUCLÉ FOR CURLY HAIR

If you can find a 100 per cent wool one, you are lucky, as most bouclé yarns have a tiny synthetic fibre running through them to add strength. This also means that the 'curls' will remain and do not get 'pulled' straight in time.

MOHAIR FOR STRAIGHT HAIR

Mohair knitting yarn is great at imitating hair as it is literally 'hairy'. It can be unsuitable for very young children as everything ends up in their mouths. Again, as with the bouclé yarn, you may only find yarn with a little added synthetic fibre to give it strength. The other advantage is that this is the best hair to be brushed. I use mohair to crochet the base for hair to be knotted onto, especially if I'm using bouclé for the hair, though you will need to match the colour.

MERINO OR ALPACA TOPS

These unspun strands of wool work less well if you use them on large dolls as long, hanging hair, as they pull apart easily. However, I like using them to make tight short curls. It is quite labour-intensive as each strand needs to be twisted and sewn into place, but well worth it. They also work for the smaller dolls' house people.

ORDINARY KNITTING YARN

You can, of course, use ordinary knitting yarn in any colour you like. I have seen some fantastic dolls made with multicoloured hair.

NATURAL SHEEP LOCKS

Long or short strands of natural sheep locks work well as hair. I love Teeswater and Wensleydale as they have long, soft and lustrous locks. Though they are mostly white, they can be dyed too.

There are many other options, not featured in this book, such as using fake fur or sheepskin pieces that can be sewn into place.

FELTING WOOL

Needle felting is useful in doll-making for shaping heads and for making eyes and mouths. You will only need wisps of eye- and mouth-coloured wool (my all-time favourites are wool batts instead of tops) and a fine or medium felting needle.

CREATIVE REUSE

I am a great believer in using what you have already – some things you may not even know you have. Here are a few things that you can 'upcycle' and turn into clothes and accessories for your dolls. Sometimes we have woollen clothes but annoyingly we have felted them by accident or they simply don't fit anymore or, worse still, the moths have been at them. I dislike throwing items away, especially when they are not even fit to give to a charity shop or pass on to somebody else. Or maybe you just cannot part with them but their use is questionable otherwise.

If you have such items consider that sleeves can become hats, other parts can become clothes, blankets, pillows or similar.

Knitted or woollen socks: in my house we have a notorious 'odd sock syndrome' and though my children now just wear odd socks (which actually makes the problem worse) occasionally I end up with a sock that is just odder than others! Socks make great hats for dolls – the rib at the top may fit a doll's head and the toe part makes a lovely pouch or sleeping bag to keep a doll warm and cosy.

Skills

Needle felting

If you have never needle felted before, please make sure you read the following notes carefully. Felting needles were created during the Industrial Revolution, so needle felting is a relatively new craft. The process itself is not much different from the ancient process of wet felting – where motion, water, soap and heat create the felting – and the result is the same: wool that is soft and fluffy becomes matted, shrinks in size and becomes firm. With the help of a felting needle we can felt wool in a far more targeted and detailed way. Needle felting in this book is used to create the Featured Needle Felted Head (see p96) and as an option to making the dolls' house people. It is by no means essential to making the dolls in this book.

To needle felt you need at least one felting needle of a medium gauge #38 (a finer needle #40 might be useful too, but not essential) and a felting mat. As long as you use wool batts as recommended in the materials section at the beginning of each project, you will be able to needle felt. It does not require any specialist skill other than stabbing the needle in and out of the wool in a straight line. The tiny notches at the end of the needle will tangle up the wool fibres on the way in. Continuous stabbing will result in the fibres getting 'knitted' tighter and tighter together, therefore firming the shape. In the process you will be able to shape and sculpt the wool. The reduction of the size takes place where you stab with the needle. You will be able to attach either more loose wool or wool shapes to an existing shape and how to do this will be covered in the individual projects.

You will also be able to use the felting needle and tiny amounts of wool to add facial features to the dolls. Again, what you will have to do is explained in the individual project. The movement of the needle remains the same, in that you stab into the shape in a straight way in and out. Please be aware that the felting needles are very sharp, so be careful not to stab yourself and keep them in a safe place away from children. When not in use, place them in a secure container.

Making a cord by 'twizzeling' yarn

Cords are great to use as the tie on a hat or a dress, as used for the Tomke doll (see p67), or when you can't find a ribbon of the right colour or width. They are easy to make and once you get the hang of it you'll find other uses for them too.

YOU WILL NEED
Approximately 3m (10ft) of double knitting yarn, which will turn into about 68cm (27in) of cord.

TIP
Making a cord requires more yarn than you might imagine – as a guide, multiply the length of cord you want by four and a half times.

Double your yarn up and knot the two loose ends. Then either ask somebody to hold one end or secure it on a door handle or with a drawing pin on a wall or door. Then twist the yarn in the same direction keeping the tension tight, making sure the other end is secure.

1. It sometimes works faster if you use a pencil: insert at the end you are twisting and spin the pencil.
2. After a while you will see that the yarn wants to curl up on itself. At this point stop twisting, reach into the centre of the twisted yarn and fold it in half. Let it 'twizzle' and just smooth over any lumps. Secure with an overhand knot at either end.
3. If you need to make this length into two or more, mark the length by putting two knots and cut between the knots. The cord will unwind itself if you let it.

Useful techniques

There are a number of sewing stitches that are used in this book. I love hand sewing and am no friend of a sewing machine. However, most projects are suitable to be sewn by machine, so feel free to use what suits you. If you are sewing by hand, these are the stitches used in the book.

RUNNING STITCH

Use this stitch for gathering fabric when making heads and hands for your dolls. It is also useful when sewing on hair and for temporary stitches, such as tacking (basting).

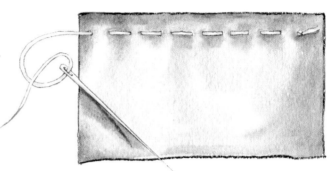

BACKSTITCH

This is a tight stitch that works for seams on bodies where you don't want the stuffing to leak out. It is also useful for making clothes and accessories.

OVER STITCH

When you can't access the other side of the fabric, over stitch is what you need. Useful for attaching heads to bodies and hands to arms, it stays on the surface only.

BLANKET STITCH

This is a great stitch for finishing the edges of fabrics so they don't fray. Blanket stitch is also decorative when used in a contrasting colour around a hat or other accessories.

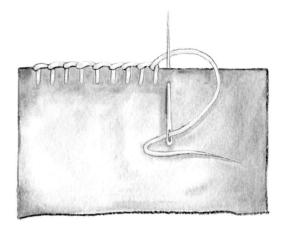

INVISIBLE OR LADDER STITCH

Use this for sealing the small holes left for stuffing. Run the stitches along the edges on either side to conceal the thread in the seam. When you pull the thread the stitches will disappear.

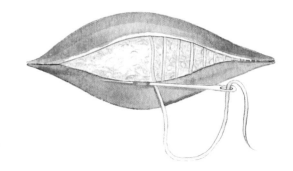

TYING A KNOT: DOUBLE OVERHAND KNOT

This is a simple overhand knot but with an extra twist. This helps to stop it slipping and undoing when you are securing a head around the base or making a featured head.

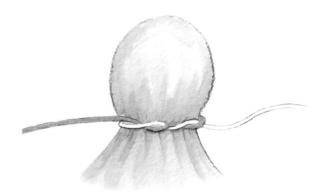

Knitting stitches

You do not need to be a proficient knitter to follow the knitted projects in this book, including Max and Mimi doll (see p55) and some accessories. The only knitting skills you need are:

- Cast on at the beginning of a project
- Cast or bind off at the end of a project
- Cast or bind off and cast on mid-project
- Knit and purl stitch
- Increase or decrease mid-row

Here is a reminder of how the different knit texture is achieved:

- Garter stitch: knit every row back and forth
- Stocking stitch: knit one row, purl one row
- Rib stitch: knit one stitch, purl one stitch, repeat till end of row, on new row put a knit stitch on top of a knit stitch and a purl stitch on top of a purl stitch.

Crochet stitches

We have used UK terms throughout this book, followed by the US term in brackets:

double crochet (single crochet)

half treble crochet (half double crochet)

treble crochet (double crochet)

The Body Shop

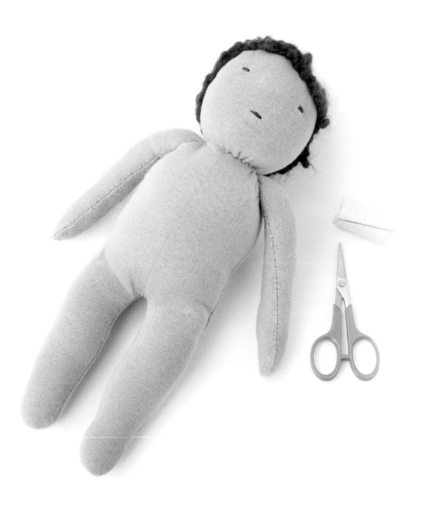

Using this Book

The Body Shop shows you different ways to create the components for your dolls: their heads, faces and hair.

Read this section first, so when you start a project you will be able to make informed decisions about which techniques you would like to use.

The Dolls (p48–77) comprises individual project instructions that show exactly how to make our dolls, but once you are happy with the techniques used you can make your own creations by combining these elements in whichever way you prefer. Of course, even if you follow the instructions, how you dress your doll and what expression your characters will have is entirely up to you – your creations will be all your own.

Dolls' Clothes and Accessories (p78–89) shows you how to re-use old garments to make into hats, trousers and dresses for your dolls. There are also knitting, crochet and sewing patterns to make clothes for most dolls.

Dolls' House Dolls and Accessories (p90–115) introduces you to a whole world in miniature, with instructions on how to make everything from a baby in a cradle to tiny satchels and even pets for the dolls' house families.

Sewing Templates (p116–125) gives you all the templates necessary for making the dolls and their clothes and accessories. They are accompanied by a guide on how to photocopy them and how they can be scaled up or down to suit your needs. We have detailed the quantities you will need to make dolls the same size as ours but feel free to experiment with size and scale. If you would like a bigger or smaller doll, all you have to do is scale up your materials too. If you have materials left over, save them for smaller projects, such as the dolls' house dolls and accessories. The smaller projects need tiny amounts of material to make another dress or tiny doll's satchel.

Frequently Asked Questions (p126) will answer questions you may have about making dolls and how best to care for them.

Making the Dolls' Bodies

You may find that I work in an unorthodox way when it comes to sewing. As mentioned before, I am not a dressmaker nor have I ever followed a pattern. I have always designed my own creations and that includes the dolls too. However, there are a few important points you need to adhere to:

- Please make sure that when cutting body shapes out of stockinette and velour that the grain of the fabric goes from top to bottom, which means the stretch is from side to side (see p16).
- Remember to pay extra attention when using double-knit stockinette as there is a wrong and a right side

(see p16). The right side should look like stocking stitch, the wrong side like a garter or purl stitch.

- Sew the body together with a tight small backstitch (see p23). It is essential that the seams are strong and will resist tight stuffing and rough handling.

Stuffing the Bodies

Max and Mimi, Hannes and Hannah, Tomke and Peter and Fenja and Felix Dolls

There are many ways to stuff the dolls, depending on how soft or hard you would like them to be. I prefer mine fairly firm, but not too hard. A long pointed stick (but not too sharp) is a great help when stuffing the dolls' extremities. This can be a 5–8mm (US8–11) knitting needle, a pencil or similar pointed utensil.

I like it when the dolls can bend their arms and legs and so I tend to stuff the arms, body and legs separately, making sure there is a small gap between each stuffed part.

Stuffing the legs

Start with the legs and add as much wool as you can, compressing the wool down as you go, filling the whole leg. Use less wool overall if you prefer your dolls to be soft. Use your pointy stick to get right into the foot area so there are no empty spaces. The stuffing wool I use (South German Merino wool batts) is ideal for creating a solid finish as well as a softer one, as the wool is one continuous soft shape and won't feel lumpy later on. Make sure both legs are stuffed with the same amount. If you want to be extra precise you could weigh the wool before stuffing one leg, then allocate the same weight of wool for the second leg.

Stuffing the torso

Again, you have options. You can just stuff the wool in or roll a firm oblong shape to fit inside the doll. It needs to be large enough to fit snugly without causing the fabric to crease. Make sure there is a gap of stuffing between the top of the legs and the lower body. If you want to give the doll more of a distinct bottom shape, roll a much smaller ball up and put it into the back area before adding the wool for the torso. You can add weight to your doll and help your doll to sit down by filling the toe part of a stocking or a pair of tights with sand, creating a pouch. that sits in the bottom of your doll's torso:

YOU WILL NEED

Thin stockings or tights 15–20 denier
Sand 250–300g (9–11oz)

SAND POUCH

1. The finer the sand the more times you will have to double-up the stocking. Start by putting the sand into the toe part of the stocking. Then twist the top and fit over the now-filled stocking again. Repeat this process until there is no sandy residue when you pat the pouch.

2. Once you have stuffed the legs of the doll, place the sand pouch into the doll where you imagine his or her bottom to be. Then make the body filling according to the instructions and place in front of the sand pouch. You may have to squeeze the sand and wool into the right place.

Stuff the arms as you did with the legs. If, as before, you would like to be able to have movement in the arms, make sure that there is a gap along the diagonal seam at the front.

Making the Heads

In this book I use four types of head, each of which has its own benefits in terms of the skills you have to hand, the materials that are available to you and of course the final effect that you would like to create. The Simple Head is exactly as the name suggests, the easiest to make and uses the most basic materials. You can still personalise the face with eyes and mouth and even hair. The Double Layered Head has two layers of fabric covering the wool batt core making it more robust, though it is still straightforward to make. The Featured and Needle Felted Heads allow for more personalisation and are great if you have the time and equipment to do felting.

You can combine the techniques used in each head to make every creation your own, for example the Mimi doll has a featured head, but no nose. Which technique you choose depends on you and how you want your doll to look.

The Simple Head

The Double Layered Head

The Featured Head

The Featured Needle Felted Head

The Simple Head

The Simple Head is by far the easiest head to make and only requires wool batts or stuffing wool and stockinette or strong jersey material in skin colours. You will also need extra-strong thread that does not tear when pulled very tight. You will need this thread for the heads, feet and hands of all the dolls in this book.

The Simple Head

The Simple Head works well with the Romi Doll (see p51) and could also work for:
- The knitted Max and Mimi Dolls (see p55)
- The velour-bodied Hannes and Hannah Dolls (see p61)
- The Dolls' House Dolls (see p90)

YOU WILL NEED

Square of stockinette or strong jersey in desired skin colour
Cream wool batts
Extra-strong thread in a neutral white or off-white colour
Embroidery needle
Scissors
Soft pencil
Ruler

ADVANTAGES
- The top of the head is smooth (no stitches) and so can remain uncovered, say for a baby's head without hair
- Easy to make with few materials
- Can be made soft

DISADVANTAGES
- It will show creases around the neck line
- The head is always round rather than oval

1

Draw a circle on the wrong side of the stockinette. Make a small mark in the centre and measure the diameter required with a ruler to either side of the central mark. Make more marks to indicate the diameter. Use your pencil to connect the outer dots into a circle. The circle does not need to look perfect.

2

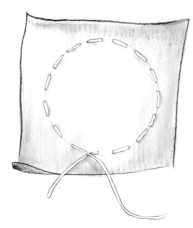

With about 50cm (20in) of your extra-strong thread, sew a running stitch on the right side, with stitches about 1cm (³/₈in) apart, until you make a full circle. Finish with a length of thread coming out on the right side next to the start of your circle.

3

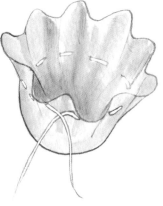

Pull both threads so that the stockinette piece makes a loose sack, making sure that the right side is on the outside (your pencil marks will be on the inside or wrong side). Put to one side for now.

4

Depending on the size of the head, use all of the measured-out wool batts and wind up into as tight a ball as you can manage.

(Tip: if you know how to needle felt you could give the wool a few stabs, which will hold the ball shape so you do not have to hold it tight in your hand).

5

Place the tight ball inside the stockinette pouch, making sure the wool ball does not pop open by pulling the thread tightly to close the circular pouch. You may have to use your finger, a knitting needle or similar, to stuff the last tufts of wool inside, as it needs to be as tight as you can manage. Then pull the thread completely tight and secure with a couple of knots using a double overhand knot (see p24).

6

If the skin-coloured fabric appears loose, you can make it tighter by adding another running stitch above the now closed and knotted thread and pulling the second one tight again, then secure with a knot as before and cut the old tie.

The head you have made will have creases around the base where you have gathered the fabric. You can minimise these once you sew the head onto the doll's body, but they will never disappear entirely. This is why this style of head works best with the simpler and softer dolls.

ADDING EYES AND MOUTH

If you wish to add details such as eyes and a mouth, you have two options:

1

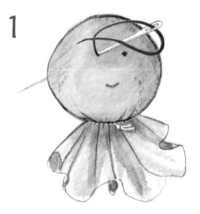

If you are giving your doll a permanent head cover such as hair or a hat, you can add the eyes by sewing into the head, securing the thread at the back and going all the way through it, adding a few stitches for eyes and mouth.

2

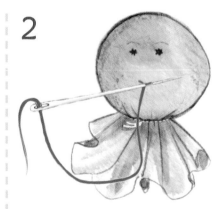

If you are planning to keep the head uncovered, you need to sew those details on superficially by just embroidering the surface (see p41).

The Double Layered Head

The advantage of this head is that you will not end up with creases around the base of the head as you put the wool in tubular gauze before covering it with the stretchy stockinette tube. Any features that you add will be embroidered on or needle felted, or you can leave the face blank.

The Double Layered Head works well with Max Doll (see p55) and could also work for:
- Tomke and Peter Dolls (p67)
- Hannes and Hannah Dolls (p61)
- Romi Doll (p51)
- Dolls' House Dolls (p90)

The Double Layered Head

YOU WILL NEED

Cotton gauze tube

Square of stockinette or strong jersey in desired skin colour

Cream wool batts

Extra-strong thread in a neutral white or off-white colour

Embroidery needle (extra long for a larger doll's head)

Embroidery thread for facial details

Felting needle and felting wool for needle felted eyes and mouth

Scissors

Soft pencil

Ruler

1

Depending on the size of the head, use all of the measured wool batts and wind up into as tight a ball as you can manage.

(Tip: if you know how to needle felt you could give the wool a few stabs, which will hold the ball shape so you do not have to hold it tight in your hand).

ADVANTAGES
- There are minimal neck creases
- The face is smooth
- Still an easy head to make

DISADVANTAGES
- Ideally you need a ready-made tube such as cotton gauze used for medical purposes. The top of the head needs to be covered by hair or a permanent hat

2

Use your length of tubular gauze and stuff the wool ball inside it. It should be a tight squeeze. Only insert the wool half way into the tube.

3

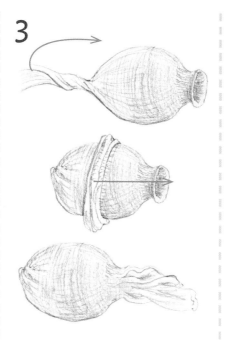

Then twist the top of the tube once or twice and pull the remainder of the gauze back over the first half which contains the wool ball. By twisting the tube you will have closed it and the second layer can be pulled tight over the first.

4

Push the wool as far as you can inside the double layer tube and tie the bottom (two ends of tube) with the extra-strong thread using the double overhand knot (see p24).

5

Sew your stockinette fabric into a tube, making sure that the seam runs along the grain of the fabric (if you are using a single-knit stockinette, make sure to sew it from the wrong side). Use backstitch (see p23) and neat, small stitches to create a strong seam. Then turn the tube inside out and fit over the head.

6

Back of the head

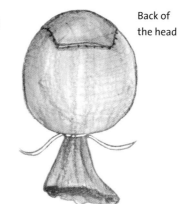

Fold the top over and sew closed as neatly as you can on what will now become the back of the head. Next tie the bottom end of the tube with your extra-strong thread but first pull the cover as tightly as possible over the head again. Use the double overhand knot (see p24) to secure.

7

You can keep the head as it is without adding eyes or a mouth or you can embroider these details or needle felt them onto the face, then sew the head onto the doll.

The Featured Head

The Featured Head is a slightly more advanced way of making a head as you will be using the extra-strong thread to tie an eye line before covering with the stockinette / jersey skin-coloured fabric. This adds indentations into the face and gives you the opportunity to add more facial details. The Featured Head is my favourite doll's head and has been used on most dolls.

The Featured Head works well with all dolls but is used specifically for Mimi Doll (see p55), Hannes Doll (see p61) and Dolls' House Doll (see p90).

The Featured Head

1

Depending on the size of the head, use all of the measured-out wool batts and wind up into as tight a ball as you can manage.

Tip: if you know how to needle felt you could give the wool a few stabs, which will hold the ball shape so you do not have to hold it tight in your hand. For this head to work it is really important that the wool ball is as firm as possible.

YOU WILL NEED

Cotton tube gauze

Rectangle-shaped stockinette or strong jersey in desired skin colour (the grain of the fabric needs to run lengthways)

Matching skin-coloured sewing thread

Embroidery needle

Cream wool batts

Extra-strong thread in a neutral white or off-white colour

Scissors

Extra long doll's needle (if circumference of head is 10cm or more)

3–5mm (C/2–H/8) crochet hook

ADVANTAGES

- The face will have a profile and contours
- Adding eyes and a mouth is easy as the proportions are pre-set
- There are minimal neck creases
- The back of the head is a nice round shape

DISADVANTAGES

- The top of the head will need to be covered either by hair or a permanent hat as there will be stitches or seams visible
- Tying the eye line can be more challenging, especially on smaller dolls

2

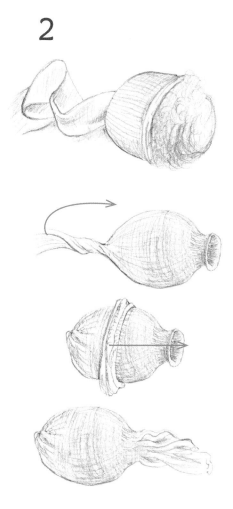

Use your length of tubular gauze and stuff the wool ball inside it. It should be a tight squeeze. Only insert the wool half way into the tube.

Then twist the top of the tube once or twice and pull the remainder of the gauze back over the first half which contains the wool ball. By twisting the tube you will have closed it and the second layer can be pulled tight over the first.

3

Push the wool as far as you can inside the double-layer tube and tie the bottom (two ends of the tube) with the extra-strong thread using a double overhand knot (see p24).

4

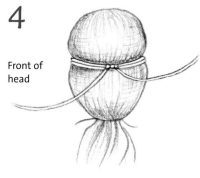

Front of head

Take a good length of your extra-strong thread and wind this round the centre of the head twice as follows:

Pull the thread as tight as you can and under tension tie a knot using the double overhand knot technique (see p24). Imagine that where you tied the knot is where the nose of the doll will be.

Move the tied thread around the head if there is a better place for the face. Now thread one of the ends of the thread onto your extra-long doll's needle (or any needle if making a small head such as for the dolls' house dolls).

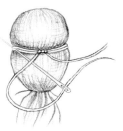

Imagine where the ear would be, following the eye line to the side of the head. Sew the thread into the fabric and around the tied eyeline to attach the eye line thread onto the side of the head.

Finish by going all the way through the head, coming out at the other side where the second ear is and securing the thread. Then repeat the process with the other end of the thread, on the other side of the head.

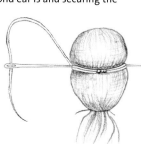

5

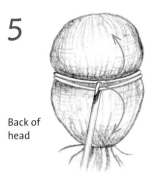

Back of head

Next use your crochet hook and separate the two parallel running threads at the back of the head by pulling one up and onto the top of the head and the other in the opposite direction onto the back neck. This may be quite hard depending on how tight your eye line thread is and you need to make sure that you will not snap the extra-strong thread or bend your crochet hook out of shape. Little movements and pushing the head with your fingers will help this process.

Moving one thread up and the other down rounds the back of the head while the front thread marks the eyeline.

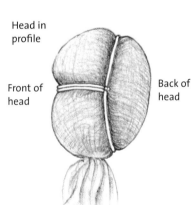

Head in profile

Front of head

Back of head

6

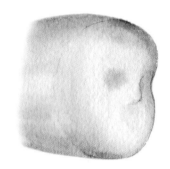

Front of head

If you wish, you can add a nose onto the face of the doll. In order to do this, roll some wool into a tight ball and sew into place (it should be where the knot is); however, if this has been slightly pulled out of place, sew the nose in line with the eye line thread into the centre of the face.

Check that the size of the nose is in proportion by stretching the jersey fabric over the face – this will give you an idea of how the face will appear later. Make the nose bigger by adding wool or make it smaller by making a new, smaller ball.

Note: You may have seen elsewhere that a small bead can be sewn onto the face instead of a wool ball for the nose. My experience has been that the hardness of the bead wears through the fabric damaging the doll's face and then the bead becomes a choking hazard.

7

Next, use your rectangle of stockinette or jersey fabric and join together into a tube along the long edge, making sure you sew it closed from the wrong side about 1cm (³⁄₈in) away from the edge. Using your skin-coloured sewing thread and a backstitch, sew the rectangle into a tube with small stitches of 3mm–5mm (¹⁄₈in–³⁄₁₆in). It needs to be a strong seam as it will slip over the head with a very tight fit.

8

Once you have done this, turn it inside out and fit over the head. Make sure the seam is at the back. It may take a little effort to squeeze the head in. If it fits easily and appears loose, take it off and sew the tube tighter by sewing another seam inside the first.

9

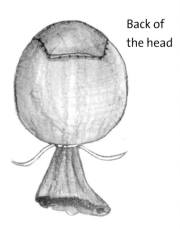

Back of the head

Once the tube fits snugly you should have the same amount of excess tube at the top and bottom. Fold the top over away from the head and forehead and sew closed on the back of the head as neatly as you can.

10

Next tie the bottom end of the tube with your extra-strong thread but first pull the cover as tight as possible over the face again. Use the double overhand knot (see p24) to secure. If necessary, tie again around the top if you need to give the cover a tighter fit. Cut the first tie once the second one is secure. You should now have a featured face with an indentation showing where the eyes will be, and if you have added a nose you should be able to see this too.

11

You can now add embroidered eyes and a mouth.

The Featured Needle Felted Head

If you already needle felt or would like to use this skill for the first time, this is a great way to make a head that is firm and has features. You are also more in control of the kind of features you would like the doll to have. Whilst in this book I mainly add features such as eyes and noses, with the felting needles, you can sculpt other details such as a chin, cheeks, forehead and cheeks. It is probably one of the easier heads to make as long as you can needle felt.

The Featured Head works well with all dolls, but has been used specifically to make Tomke Doll's face (see p72), which also has needle felted eyes and mouth.

The Featured
Needle Felted Head

YOU WILL NEED

Rectangle-shaped stockinette or strong jersey in desired skin colour (the grain of the fabric needs to run lengthways)
Matching skin-coloured sewing thread
Cream lanolin-rich wool batts (I use South German Merino, cold-washed)
Extra-strong tear-proof thread in a neutral white or off-white colour
Felting needles (medium #38 and fine #40)
Dyed felting wool for eyes, eyebrows and mouth
Scissors

ADVANTAGES
- You are in control of more facial details such as forehead, chin, mouth or nose

DISADVANTAGES
- You need to know how to needle felt and may require a little practice

1

Use about one third of the wool for the head and roll as tight as you can into a ball shape. This is best done by winding the wool up in on itself. When you only have the wispy ends left, use your medium felting needle and stab this into a ball shape to tuck them away and so securing the shape at the same time. The head shape may be more oval at this point. Use your felting needle and stab right into the centre all around.

Watch out for the needle coming out on the other side if you are holding the shape in your hand. By stabbing all over you are firming the ball up even more and you can adjust the overall shape.

2

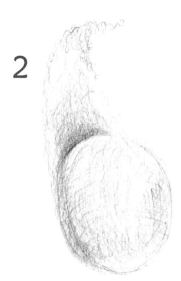

Next take another similar amount of wool batts and wrap it around the established head shape as tightly as you can. You may have to tease the wool out so it becomes more of a flat sheet as this is easier to wrap and covers more. If the original shape is more oval than round, layer the wool so it wraps around the longer part.

3

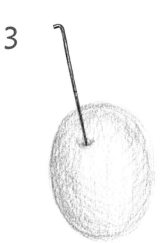

Felt the wispy ends down first, then firm up all over by stabbing the needle into the wool. By now your shape should be so firm that it becomes quite hard to stab all the way into the centre. Repeat the same wrapping process again. Leave a good amount of wool (minimum of one-tenth) to add features.

4

ADDING NEEDLE FELTED FEATURES

A young child's head has quite distinct features, such as a large forehead, small nose and mouth and chin. Firstly build up the forehead by laying strands of wool from side to side to the top of the face and felt them down. Add more to build up the shape. Then do the same with the chin but with much less wool.

For the nose add a small ball of wool and make sure that the bridge of the nose is a curved shape running from the tip of the nose into the forehead.

Needle felt two indentations just above the nose where the eyes will be.

5

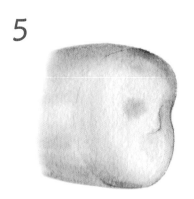

If you are uncertain as to the finished look, use your stockinette and lay it over the face, pulling it tight. It will give you a really good idea of what the face will look like and you can use that to inform you where to add more wool or felt the face down.

6

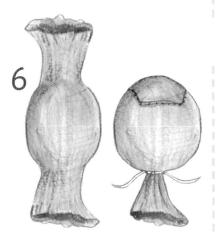

When you are happy, sew the stockinette fabric, right sides together, into a tube, allowing about 1cm (³⁄₈in) for the seam. The grain of the fabric needs to run lengthways, the stretch from side to side.

Turn the tube right side out and fit over the head. Make sure the seam is at the back. Once the tube fits snugly, fold

7

the top over away from the front of the head and sew closed on the back of the head as neatly as you can.

Next pull the cover as tightly as possible and tie the bottom end of the tube with extra-strong thread using the double overhand knot (see p24) to secure.

Faces

For the face you have several options: you can leave the face unmarked or without any features; have minimal features such as embroidered eyes and mouth; or needle felt these features, keeping them small and with little detail. For example, eyes are just a couple of stitches back and forth or a round small dot needle felted into place; or you can add more detail. If you want more features, add freckles by using a fine liner pen and just make tiny dots. You can use a non-oily crayon to blush the cheeks (or even use real blusher).

You can also make the eyes and mouth more distinct and real-looking by embroidering these more elaborately. There is a danger of them looking 'cartoonish'. Needle felted eyes and mouths may be a better option for keeping them subtle.

I have kept the dolls' faces relatively plain with 'open faces', as I believe it adds to the charm of the doll but also, as mentioned at the beginning of the book, it allows children to put their own imagination into the facial expressions of the dolls.

The eyes need to be half way between the top of the forehead and the bottom of the chin. The nose is just below that imaginary line between the eyes. In a young child's face the eyes are far apart and this is quite a distinct feature to make any face appear young and innocent.

Fitting the head
(for all dolls except Dolls' House Dolls)

1

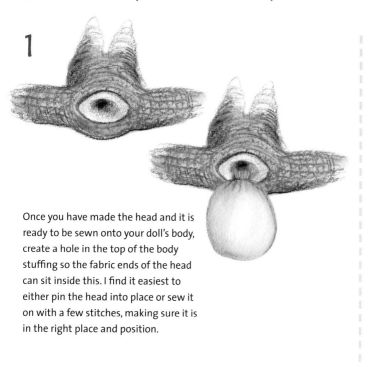

Once you have made the head and it is ready to be sewn onto your doll's body, create a hole in the top of the body stuffing so the fabric ends of the head can sit inside this. I find it easiest to either pin the head into place or sew it on with a few stitches, making sure it is in the right place and position.

2

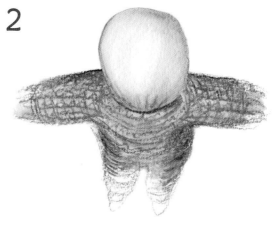

Sew the head on with an invisible stitch always going in and out of the doll's body's fabric and in and out of the doll's head base, as far down towards the tie as possible. Use thread that matches the colour of the stockinette. Diligent sewing pays off and going round the base of the head three to four times, sewing the two parts together, will keep it secure.

3

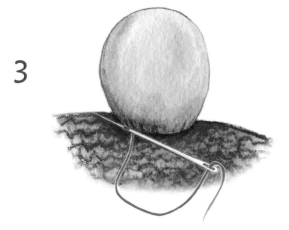

At the very end wind the thread around the neck tightly two times to pull the neck line in a little and make it more distinct.

Then make a few more stitches as before and tidy the thread away at the back of the head.

For the Romi Doll (Simple Doll) and the Dolls' House Dolls, follow the specific instructions in the respective project sections.

Hair
CROCHETED CAP AND CARPET-KNOTTED HAIR

The crochet cap and knotted strands method is quite labour-intensive and uses up more hair yarn (for long hair) and sewing thread than you may imagine. To make a large doll – such as Tomke Doll – with a 9cm (3¾in) diameter head and with long shoulder-length hair, you will need up to 100g (3½oz) yarn. Mohair and bouclé can be quite expensive and I have often found that making long hair in this way costs more than the making of the entire doll. It is however my preferred style of hair, as the crocheted cap can hide the stockinette scalp, and it seems to be the most robust way of making a doll with long hair. You can leave just the cap for short hair and there are mohair yarns that can be brushed so that short hair is created this way. You can also knot shorter strands to the cap for a short hairstyle.

YOU WILL NEED

Mohair or bouclé yarn (you can mix yarns either in colour or texture; always use the mohair for the cap if you are mixing textures, for better coverage)
Sewing thread to match the hair colour
Small crochet hook, no larger than 4mm (G/6)
Sewing needle

Crocheting with mohair or bouclé yarn can be quite tricky as it is very hairy and you often cannot see the stitch you need to crochet into. The upside is that you can also not see any imperfections, so do not worry too much about always crocheting perfectly into each stitch. A further disadvantage is that undoing anything crocheted, especially with a relatively small crochet hook, will be almost impossible.

1

Use your wool and crochet a chain so that it is long enough to reach from ear to ear across the top of the head.

2

Then turn and crochet the next rows in a half treble (half double US) until the piece when folded in half widthways fits the doll's head like a cap. The cap needs to be a tight fit onto the doll's head and once big enough will be stretched and sewn into place so that there are no bulges.

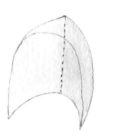

Crocheted rectangle folded in half and sewn together down one side

Bear this in mind when checking if the cap is large enough. Once the rectangle is big enough, crochet or sew one of the long sides together (see diagram above).

3

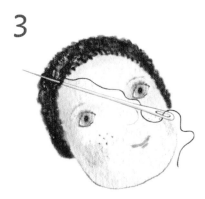

Next, fit onto the doll's head and sew it into place just around the face with an over stitch pulled tight so that the thread disappears into the mohair. Keep checking that it is in the right position and symmetrical. Use pins to hold in place if needed.

The seam of the cap can either be on top of the head like a middle parting (see above) or at the back of the head – it depends which way the cap fits best.

4

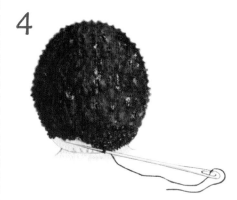

Make sure that the cap reaches all the way down the back of the head into the nape of the neck, covering the seam of the head.

Once the cap is fitted, sew in small neat stitches all across the head to secure the rest of the cap. This is a great opportunity to close up any gaps in the crocheted cap that may have been created by pulling it.

Continue using a cross stitch (see above where stitches are indicated in contrasting colour for visibility only): the stitches need to blend in with the cap colour) for this step. You may have to re-thread your needle three or four times. If you are making this doll for a younger child, the hair is one of the parts of dolls that will get handled a lot, so the cap needs to be fixed very securely to the head.

KNOTTING STRANDS OF WOOL ONTO THE CAP

You will need to use your crochet hook for this process and also to decide the length of the hair. If you are making short hair (short all over) then the strands you will cut will all be the same size for all around the head.

If you are making longer hair you can make a layered hairstyle again by having all strands the same length, but due to the nature of the hair reaching less down the back of the head if knotted higher up, the hair lower down will appear longer.

This is an easier hairstyle and saves you working out where to put longer or shorter strands, but will be messier and less versatile if you want to make pony tails or bunches (pig tails) later.

Bear in mind that a single strand will be doubled when using this method and you will need to have a long enough strand to accommodate the doubling up and the knotting. Therefore it is easier to aim for a longer strand and cut it shorter later on, than to start out with too short a strand.

1

Start by cutting several strands of hair at the same time. I do this by using a template of cardboard and wrapping the wool around it (see above) or measuring one strand and then using this one to measure the others against it. You will create a large round of wool, so you need to cut the loop at the top and bottom into individual strands, or just at one edge if you need longer strands of hair .

2

You will be making a carpet knot to attach the hair. (see right).

CARPET KNOT

1. Insert the crochet hook into the cap, catching a couple of stitches.
2. Fold the strand in half and use the hook to pull the strand through the loop of the cap, creating a new loop with the hair strand.
3. Use the hook to take the ends through the new loop and pull tight with your fingers.
4. You have created two strands of hair attached to the cap.

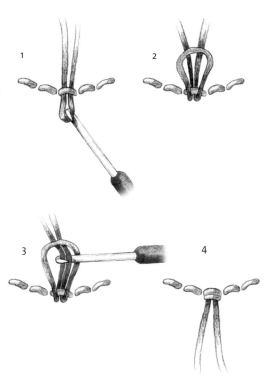

3

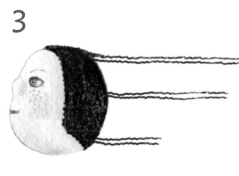

Start by knotting the hair onto the bottom of the head, working your way up. That way you don't have to keep moving the strands out of the way to add more. It will also show you what the ultimate length of hair could be. Remember you can always cut it shorter; however, equally you do not want to waste precious hair yarn. You will need longer strands of hair at the top of the head (see above) as these strands have a longer area to cover.

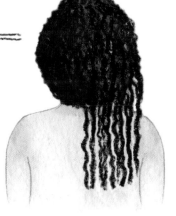

You do not need to cover the whole of the scalp as you will end up with a huge shock of hair. I recommend spacing the strands of hair out every 1cm–2cm (³/₈in – ³/₄in) to start with and then add more if needed. If your mohair yarn is finer you may need to add more strands; if it is a chunky yarn you will need less.

You can make a fringe or have a parting, or have the hair falling into the face or straight back over the head.

My daughters have always loved making different hairstyles for their dolls and long hair in a doll was a definite attraction for some of them.

MAKING TIGHT CURLS

This method of sewing felting wool tops onto the head gives the doll lovely short and tight curly hair and I have found it the longest lasting and neatest way, especially as it is quite hard to make short curls in other ways. Admittedly it is labour-intensive, but well worth it! You need long strands of wool tops that you split into thinner strands, twist and sew onto the head as you go along. Wool tops are strands of unspun wool and they are usually very soft if you opt for Merino, alpaca or even mohair.

YOU WILL NEED

25g (¾oz) of alpaca or wool tops (for an 8cm (3¼in) diameter head)
Sewing needle
Sewing thread to match

1

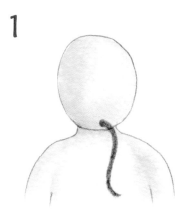

Once your doll's head is finished (including the face) and sewn onto the doll's body, separate your wool tops lengthwise into 1cm (³⁄₈in)-thick strands. Try working with as long a strand as you can manage but no more than 50cm (20in).

Secure your thread at the back of the head and sew the beginning of the wool strand onto the back of the doll's head near the neck line.

2

Once the strand of wool is secure, twist the whole of the strand, pulling approximately 20cm (7½in) away from the head – keep twisting in the same direction until it starts to curl up on itself.

Once it does that, sew the curled-up part onto the head, covering a small area.

Then repeat with more of the wool strands. It is really important that you sew the hair on well and go over it several times, always pulling the thread tight.

3

You will create a 'frame' of hair to outline the face and then fill in the gaps. You can make a slight curve round the side of the head where the ear would be.

4

The head and therefore the hair is one of the most handled parts of the doll and it needs to be totally secure. Continue creating the frame of the hair around the neckline, side of the head and the forehead and then fill in the area on the top and back of the head until you have a dense cover with no fabric showing through. At the very end finish off by sewing over the whole head again, checking that the wool curls are secured.

Back of the head

SEWING STRANDS OF HAIR ONTO THE HEAD FOR SHORT OR LONG HAIR

This style has been used in many traditional Waldorf dolls and is perfect for creating long flowing locks as well as shorter trimmed styles.

1. Remember that each strand will be only half as long once attached to the head as you will sew it on in the middle of the strand.

2. Start by sewing each folded strand onto the head making sure that the needle and thread catches the bent part of the strand so the hair doesn't slip out. Use a backstitch for extra security.

YOU WILL NEED

50g (1¾oz) double knitting wool, Teeswater or Wensleydale, or
100g (3½oz) Aran weight wool (quantity depends how long you want to make your hair)
Sewing needle
Sewing thread to match

1

Start by cutting several strands of hair at the same time. I do this by using a template of cardboard and wrapping the wool around it (see above) or measuring one strand and then using this one to measure the others against it.

2

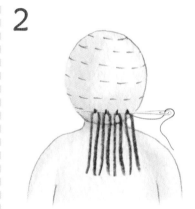

Start sewing strands of wool onto the base of the head and work your way systematically up towards the crown of the head. Once you add a new layer, the stitches of the one underneath will be hidden. It is important that your thread is as close to the colour of hair as possible.

3

The last layer will become a fringe if you choose to have one. Trim the hair at the very end if need be.

Note: The advantages of making hair this way is that you will not have to crochet a cap and use a large amount of wool and time to knot each strand onto the cap. The disadvantage is that fewer hairstyles can be made with this style as the strands are more attached to the head.

The Dolls

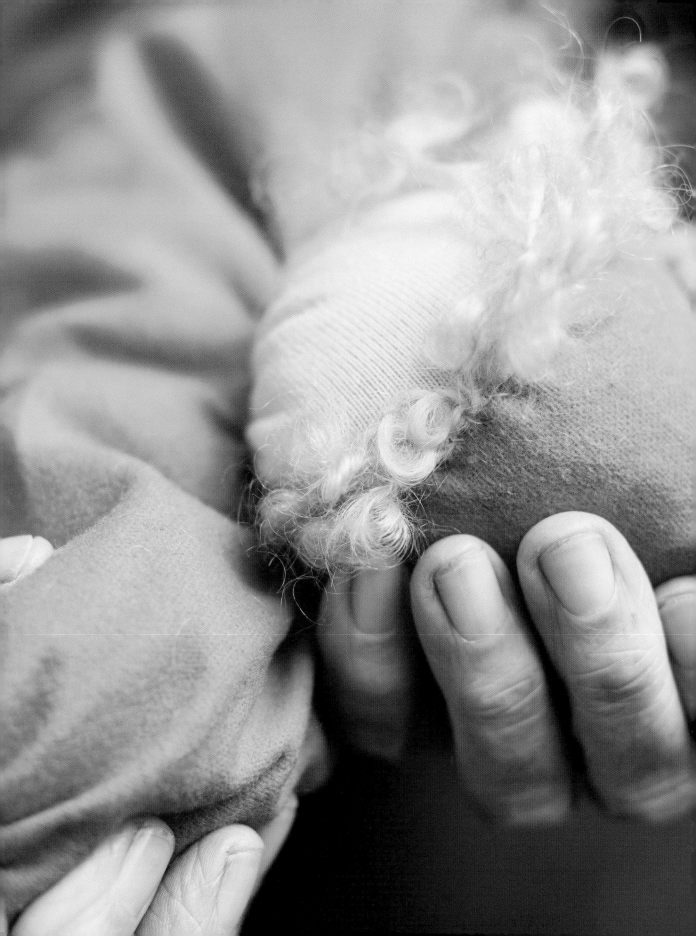

Romi Doll The First and Last Doll

I like to think of this simple doll as The First and Last Doll. It certainly was my eldest daughter's first doll and the first doll I made for her. I got so much pleasure from making such a simple little doll, and she took to it instantly as a toddler and cuddled and loved it for many years. I also know of people who have made a similar doll as a last doll for their parent at the end of their life where hands aged by years have held and squeezed their doll with much the same affection. Perhaps you are making this doll as a first or last doll for somebody?

YOU WILL NEED

TRIANGULAR BODY
55cm x 47cm (21½in x 18½in) of brushed cotton or flannelette to make two triangles, each measuring 54cm x 35cm x 35cm (21in x 13½in x 13½in)
Matching sewing thread
50g (1¾ oz) of wool nepps or wool stuffing for the body
Sewing needle

MATCHING HAT
25cm x 27cm (9½in x 10½in) of flannelette to match the body

HEAD
15g (½oz) stuffing wool
22cm x 22cm (8½in x 8½in) skin-coloured single or double knit stockinette
1m (40in) extra-strong thread
Sewing needle
Few strands bouclé yarn in the colour of your choice for hair

Finished Measurements
28cm (11in) from bottom of triangle to top of head (not hat) and the head is 8cm–8.5cm (3¼in–3½in) in diameter

1

Body

Cut the two triangles from the template (see p117) and sew together from the wrong side along the two shorter sides of the shape and the longer side, keeping an opening of 5cm (2in) at the middle for the head to fit in later (see right).

If you are cutting the fabric so it folds in half at the top (saves sewing the longer side of the triangle), you will need to cut a neck hole into the top of about 5cm (2in) length before sewing up the two shorter sides (see below).

Cut edge   Neck hole

Folded edge   Neck hole

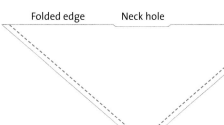

2

Turn the triangular shape inside out. Use a pointed stick to push the two sharper corners out properly.

Double up your sewing thread for extra strength if you are sewing by hand. Use a backstitch and keep the stitches neat and small.

The seam allowance is only 5mm (³/₁₆in) wide, so once you have sewn around the body go over the seam again, this time using a blanket stitch (see p24) to prevent the edges fraying and to add strength.

3

Smooth the fabric as much as you can on one side where the sharper point is and knot as far down to the end as possible. This will be one hand. Repeat on the other side. You may find that the fabric is quite stiff and it is hard to pull the knot through.

4

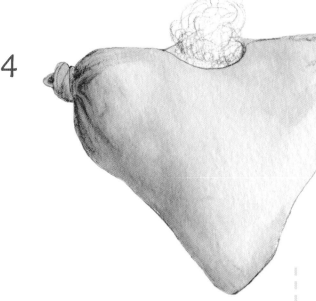

Fill the body with either the stuffing wool or the wool nepps to your preferred firmness. I keep mine soft and squishy, and 50g (1¾oz) of stuffing will achieve that.

5

Head

Make a simple head (see p31).

6

Hair

Fold the yarn into 5cm (2in)-long loops, spread across the forehead and sew them down so they are secure. You can cut the loops off or leave them; either way the hair will only be peeping out from under the hat.

7

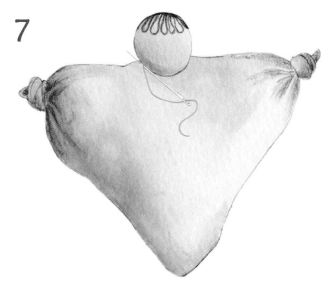

Sew the head onto the top of the triangular body, hiding the stockinette end inside the wool and sewing closed any open sides of the triangle using an invisible stitch (see p24).

8

Fold line

This template is not actual size

Hat

Cut out the hat using the template (see p117) and sew right-sides together along the straight, long side with a 1cm (³⁄₈in) seam allowance and backstitch. Turn the hat inside out.

9

Fit the hat and sew onto the head, starting at the back and folding the edge in by 1cm (³⁄₈in). You may want to pin the hat down to keep it in place, especially if it is slightly large. Gather any hat excess at the back of the head rather than around the front.

Sew the back of the hat onto the top of the body (nape of the neck) as though it was attached to it. Then sew all around the base of the hat straight into the head using a neat invisible stitch.

Max and Mimi The Knitted Doll

The first time I came across a knitted doll I saw the opportunities to open doll-making to all kinds of people who are not too keen on sewing. I loved the idea that suddenly doll-making could be so much more achievable and possible to a wider audience, including younger children. I truly hope that many people will make one.

This doll is a great one for beginners, including children. The knitting pattern is straightforward: you need to be able to do a knit stitch (every row a knit row), cast off and on in mid row and at the end or beginning of a row. You can choose the yarns to either create a uniform body or make the top half from a different colour to the bottom half. The added advantage of this doll is that it is super soft and does not need dressing, therefore making it a perfect first doll too.

Mimi Doll (see below left) was made using two types of yarn for the body and a Featured Head (see p35) without a nose. Max Doll (below right) is made with the Double Layered Head (see p33).

YOU WILL NEED

KNITTED BODY

100g (3½oz) double knitting yarn 100% wool for Max
50g (1¾oz) double knitting yarn in red and
50g (1¾oz) multi-colour yarn for Mimil
40–50g (1½–1¾oz) stuffing wool
4mm (US6) knitting needles
Darning needle

DOUBLE LAYERED HEAD FOR MAX

40g (1½oz) stuffing wool
3.5cm (1⅜in) cotton tubular gauze
Stockinette 15cm long x 20cm wide (5¾in x 7½in)
Embroidery thread for eyes and mouth

FEATURED HEAD FOR MIMI

23cm x 23cm (9in x 9in) double or single knit stockinette square
50g (1¾oz) stuffing wool
Felting needle and felting wool for eyes and mouth

HAIR

100g (3½oz) double knitting yarn

HANDS

8cm x 8cm (3¼in x 3¼in) stockinette per hand
6cm (2¼in) diameter circle drawn onto inside, stitch with running stitch and pull tight
2g (¹⁄₁₆oz) or pinch of wool to fill

FEET

10cm x 10cm (4in x 4in) stockinette per foot
8cm (3¼in) diameter circle drawn onto inside
3–4g (¹⁄₃₂oz –¹⁄₈oz) or a pinch of wool to fill

TIP
Two strands of the double knitting yarn are knitted together for these dolls, so you may wish to use chunky-weight yarn instead, keeping the same size needles. Be sure to make a tension square to check your gauge.

Finished Measurements

38cm (15in) tall

To knit the body

Tension: 10cm x 10cm (4in x 4in) 18 sts in garter stitch (knit every row).

The body needs to be knitted quite densely so we are using a small needle and two strands of yarn: the stitches need to be tight so that the stuffing does not peep through.

- Cast on 44 stitches.
- Knit the next 20 rows in garter stitch (knit each row).

- 21st row: Knit 18 sts, cast off (bind off) 8 (end with 18 sts on each side).
- 22nd row: Knit 18 sts, cast on 8 sts, knit 18 sts (44 sts).
- Knit the next 19 rows in garter stitch.
- 42nd row: Cast off 14 sts, knit remaining 30 sts to the end.
- 42nd row: Cast off 14 sts, knit remaining 16 sts, then cast on 14 sts (30 sts).
- 44th row: Knit over newly cast-on stitches to the end of the row, then cast on another 14 sts (44 sts).
- Knit the next 8–9 rows in garter stitch (more rows will make the upper body longer).
- Next row: Change to the new colour (here multi-coloured yarn) now. If you are making the doll in the same colour, continue with the same yarn. Knit this and the following 8–9 rows in garter stitch.

Legs

Next you will be working each leg separately. You can either do this by using a stitch-holder and just knitting one leg at a time or you can knit both legs simultaneously by dividing your leftover yarn into two and using one part for each leg. Here are the instructions to knit both legs simultaneously:

- 1st row: Knit 22 sts with the original yarn, then knit the next 22 sts with a new strand of yarn on the same needle.
- 2nd row: Knit 22 sts with the new strand of yarn, then knit the next 22 sts with the original yarn.
- Continue like this for the next 50–56 rows – depending on how long you would like the legs to be.

- If you are knitting one leg at a time, put 22 sts on a stitch-holder, knit the remaining 22 sts back and forth for 50–56 rows (make a note of the number of rows), then cast off and put the sts from the stitch-holder back onto your needle and knit the same number of rows as the other leg and cast off.

This is the shape of the knitted body you will be working towards.

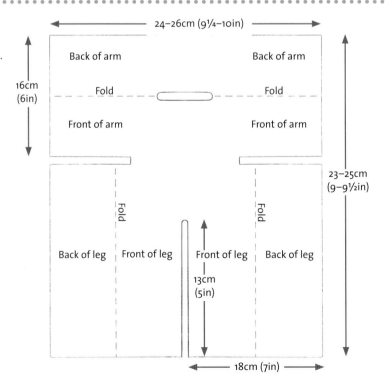

MAKING SOFT DOLLS   56

1

Making up the body

Lay the knitted shape flat. Fold one leg in from the side to the centre and sew up on the inside leg, starting at the foot end – make sure to have the wrong side on the outside as the whole shape will be turned inside out later. Only sew the sides together as far as the inside of the leg will go. You will have a little left at the top, which will be part of the lower body. Then repeat on the other leg.

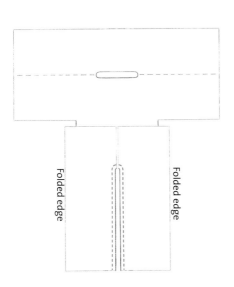

2

Sew the two extra parts that you left at the top of the legs together. The whole of the lower body part is now complete, looking like a pair of trousers.

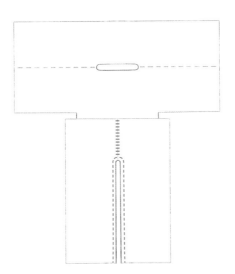

3

Fold the whole length of the arms down so that the neck hole is at the top. Sew the seams under the arm together and as with the legs sew the extra length to the top of the 'trouser' top. Once all the seams are sewn together and the yarn ends have been tidied away, turn the whole shape inside out. The back of the doll is where all the leg and arm seams meet; the front is just one continuous part.

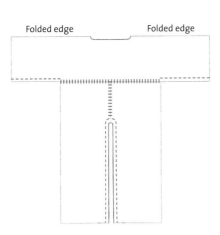

4

Hands and feet

Cut two 8 x 8cm (3¼ x 3¼in) squares from the stockinette / skin-coloured jersey for the hands and two 10 x 10cm (4 x 4in) squares for the feet.

Draw a circle with a 6cm (2¼in) diameter for the hands and 8cm (3¼in) diameter for the feet onto the square piece of fabric.

5

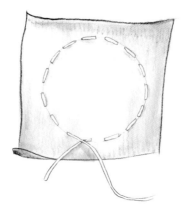

Using your extra-strong thread, follow the line by making a running stitch all around it.

Make sure you start and finish the thread on the not-drawn-on side. The stitches should be about 1cm (³⁄₈in) long and the same distance apart.

6

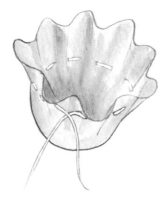

Take 2g (¹⁄₁₆oz) of stuffing wool (for the hands) and 4g (¹⁄₈oz) of stuffing wool (for the feet) and wind into a tight little ball shape. Pull the two ends of the extra-strong thread so that you create a little pouch (the drawn line should be on the inside and the ends of the thread on the outside).

7

Pull the thread tight with the wool ball inside and secure the thread with a knot. Make two feet and two hands in this way.

8

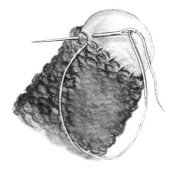

Sew the feet onto the end of the leg and hands onto the ends of the arms using matching thread. They look nice if they are partially hidden inside the 'trouser' leg or sleeve. Use an over stitch and make sure to hide the wrinkly parts that are caused by pulling the thread. Go over the seam a couple of times to make sure the feet and hands are sewn on well.

9

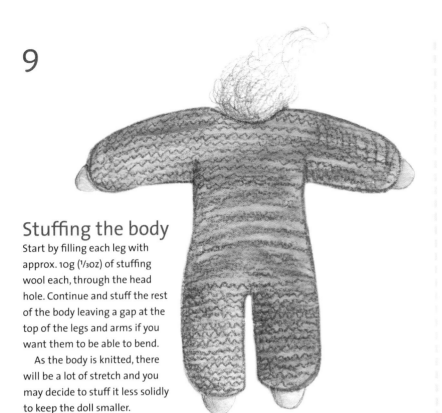

Stuffing the body

Start by filling each leg with approx. 10g (⅓oz) of stuffing wool each, through the head hole. Continue and stuff the rest of the body leaving a gap at the top of the legs and arms if you want them to be able to bend.

As the body is knitted, there will be a lot of stretch and you may decide to stuff it less solidly to keep the doll smaller.

10

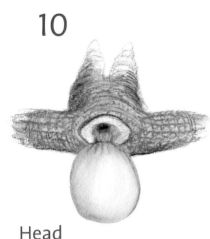

Head

Make the head using the Featured Head method (see p35) or Double Layered Head (see p33). Sew the head onto the doll's body. Make sure that you tuck the ends of the head right into the wool stuffing so it cannot be felt through the knitted body.

11

Face

Add embroidered features such as eyes and a mouth or needle felt them onto the doll's face.

12

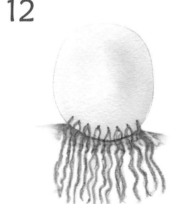

Hair

Use either the method of crocheting a cap and then carpet knotting the hair to it (blond bouclé hair) or sew the hair on (turmeric-coloured curls) – see right and see the hair section (p43) for either method.

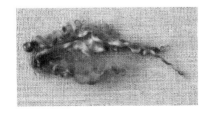

Hannes and Hannah Dolls The Velour Doll

Hannes is a real doll in real life. In fact he was my son's first doll who found his way into our family when my son was only a toddler. I saw an advert on a German website where a Kindergarten was to be closed down and one of their dolls called Hannes was looking for a new home. Well, that was it! The deal was sealed and Hannes arrived safely in the post. He definitely looked loved with his short blond hair and slightly worn blue body. I told my son that we now had to look after Hannes as he had lost his other home in Germany. He was much loved and still exists!

The red Hannah doll is almost the same as her brother Hannes, but with a simpler shape as if wearing a dress or sleep-suit and she has a plain face.

YOU WILL NEED

BODY
50g (1¾oz) stuffing wool (for Hannah Doll I used 30g [1oz] wool nepps to make a soft, squishy body)
Velour (Nicki) fabric (blue for Hannes and red for Hannah)
1. Larger body piece (A) 28cm wide x 28cm long (11in x 11in)
2. Smaller body piece (B) 16cm wide x 23cm long (6in x 9in) (total piece 44cm wide x 28cm long [17in x 11in])
Sewing thread to match the velour fabric

HAT
20cm x 25cm (7½in x 9½in) velour (Nicki) fabric (blue for Hannes and red for Hannah)

HAIR
Embroidery thread in the colour of your choice for hair

HANDS
2 pieces 5cm x 5cm (2in x 2in) skin-coloured stockinette to match the head
Sewing thread to match the skin-coloured stockinette
1g (¹⁄₃₂oz) stuffing wool

HANNES: FEATURED HEAD
16cm x 16cm (6in x 6in) double or single knit stockinette square
20–25g (¾oz) wool for stuffing
50cm (20in) of 3.5cm (1³⁄₈in) tubular cotton gauze
2m (6½ft) extra-strong thread
Sewing thread matching skin colour
Sewing needles
Long doll's needle to fit a 5cm–6.5cm (2in–2½in)-diameter head
Wisps of black and red felting wool
Medium or fine felting needle

HANNAH: DOUBLE LAYERED HEAD
16cm x 16cm (6in x 6in) double or single knit stockinette square
20–25g (¾oz) stuffing wool
50cm (20in) of 3.5cm (1³⁄₈in) tubular cotton gauze
1m (40in) extra-strong thread
Sewing thread matching skin colour
Sewing needles

Finished Measurements

25cm (9½in) tall

HANNES DOLL

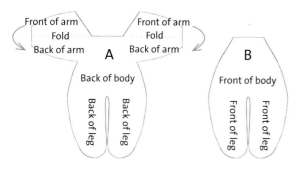

HANNAH DOLL

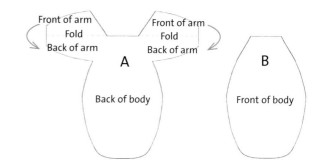

HANNES DOLL

HANNAH DOLL

1

Body

Follow the templates in the book (see p118–120) and cut out the pattern pieces A and B for Hannes with two legs and Hannah with a round pouch shape instead of legs.

Fold the arms over on the fold line as indicated on the pattern piece A. Sew the two body parts together wrong sides out, starting under the arms, working around the side and lower body and finishing underneath the other arm.

Double up your sewing thread for extra strength if you are sewing by hand. Use a backstitch and keep the stitches neat and small.

The seam allowance is only 5mm (³/₁₆in) wide, so once you have sewn around the body go over the seam again, this time using a blanket stitch (see p23) to prevent the edges fraying and to add strength.

NOTE: Velour is quite hard to sew as it is soft and slippery and so care needs to be taken whilst cutting it and pinning it together. On the upside, the fabric is very forgiving as it 'swallows' up any messy stitches in its soft fluffy surface.

2

Turn the made-up body the right side out. Use an invisible thread and sew the seams from under the arm going diagonally to the top of the arm. This is the front of the doll and helps the arms to bend forward.

3

Hands

Take one of the small stockinette pieces for the hands and draw a circle of about 3cm (1¼in) diameter on the wrong side of the fabric.

4

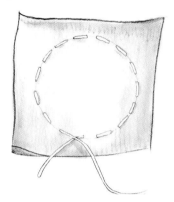

Sew a running stitch following the circle, leaving long threads at each end.

5

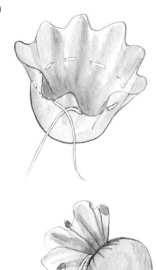

Use half the stuffing wool for the hands and roll into a tight little ball. Pull the thread so the fabric closes in, placing the wool ball inside. Pull the thread tight and secure with a double overhand knot (see p24) before sewing around the base of the hand a few times.

6

Fit the hand inside the velour body sleeve and use an invisible stitch (see p24) to sew the hand onto the arm.

Make sure that the velour fabric is folded over by a small amount to make a hem so that the edge does not show. The nature of the soft velour is that it will 'swallow' up the skin-coloured thread if you pull it tight enough.

Repeat for the second hand on the other side.

7

Stuffing the body

HANNES DOLL
Start by filling the legs – use a stick, such as a knitting needle, to make sure the wool fills the feet tightly. Then work your way up to the top of the leg. Repeat on the other side. Stuff the arms before stuffing the body. For more information about how to stuff the body see p29.

HANNAH DOLL
I have used wool nepps (tiny wool balls) to stuff her lower and upper body, adding bulk quickly while keeping the shape lofty and soft.

8

Head
For both heads follow instructions according to the Featured Head or Double Layered Head (see p33), using the quantities of materials as listed and winding the stuffing wool into a tight ball until it measures about 6.5cm (2½in) in diameter.

Then sew the head on to the body, tucking the loose ends well into the wool stuffing so they are hidden.

9

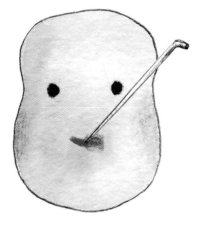 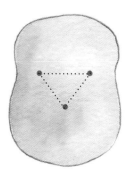

Face
You can keep the face as it is (Hannah Doll) or use needle felting for the details such as the eyes and mouth (Hannes Doll). For this you need tiny wisps of black and red wool and a medium or fine felting needle. Place tiny wisps of wool onto the area where you imagine the eyes should go (the eyes and mouth form a triangle) and felt down by concentrating the needle in one spot. The wool will be pulled in and you will be able to make a tiny black disc-shaped spot. Add more wool if you want it to be bigger; felt down more if you want to reduce the size. Repeat with the other eye and then do the same with red wool for the mouth.

10

Hair

As these dolls have a hat permanently sewn on, they don't need hair. However, you can use embroidery thread in hair colours (brown for brunette, for example) and sew a few long strands of hair onto the forehead. The important detail to remember is that you start with the embroidery thread on the top or back of the head, which will be hidden by the hat later, and that the strands of hair peep from under the hat and the beginning of each strand is invisible, hidden under the hat again.

Adding hair is by no means essential to these dolls and they look charming just with a hat. On the other hand, you may choose any other hairstyle as featured in the Hair section (see p43) instead of the permanent hat.

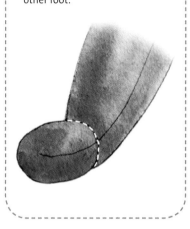

OPTIONAL EXTRA:
Give Hannes Doll more distinct feet by sewing across the top of them. Use a running stitch in the colour of his body and sew straight across, then pull it tight, go back through the foot, and secure the thread. Repeat on the other foot.

11

This template is not actual size

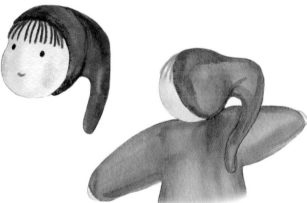

Hat

The hat for these dolls is like a tall gnome's hat and looks particularly lovely in velvet as it flops over, like a nightcap. Cut out the hat using the template (see p119). Fold the material in half and sew with a 3cm–5cm (1¼in–2in) seam allowance together from the wrong side using a backstitch along the two long sides of the hat. Go over the seam twice or finish with a blanket stitch. Turn the hat right side out. You have the option to fold the rounded edge over and secure with a running stitch before sewing the hat with the skin-coloured thread onto the head of the doll. Or you can fold the edge under as you are sewing the hat on. In any case, start sewing the hat at the neck at the back so that the hat fabric touches the body fabric and hides any head seams. Some people like adding a little wool inside the hat. That is left to your personal preference.

Tomke and Peter Doll The Stockinette Doll

These two dolls are the most detailed in the book and have a 'naked' body making them ideal to dress, which is what children love doing. Tomke Doll has a needle felted head and face whereas Peter has an embroidered face. Peter reminds me of 'Peter Püppi', the doll my grandmother made after the war for her children to play with and who is now in my family, though now a little worse for wear! Tomke is slightly taller than Peter and the way their hair has been made differs too but they are made using the same template (see p121). Peter has a smaller head and simple feet.

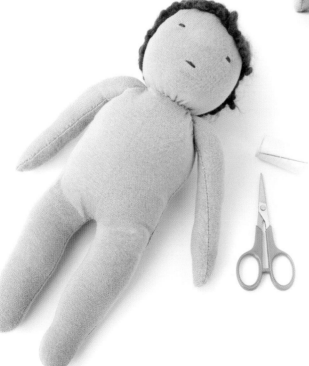

Finished Measurements

Tomke Doll: from neck to toe, 30cm (12in) – including head 37cm (14½in) – head diameter 9cm (3¾in)

Peter Doll: from neck to toe 23cm (9in) – including head 30cm (12in) – head diameter 8cm (3¼in)

YOU WILL NEED

TOMKE DOLL

BODY

85–100g (3–4oz) stuffing wool

Double knit stockinette for back and arms front and back: 56cm wide x 34cm (22in x 13in)

For front only: 16cm wide x 27cm (6in x 10½in) – total piece 72cm (28in) wide and 34cm (13in) long

Sewing thread to match

1m (40in) extra-strong thread for tying the neck

FEATURED NEEDLE FELTED HEAD

60g (2oz) wool for stuffing

Double knit stockinette 26cm x 24cm (10in x 9¼in)

Wisps of felting wool in pink, green (for the eyes), white, black and light brown
Thread

CROCHETED CAP FOR HAIR

10g (⅓oz) brown mohair yarn (chunky)

100g (3½oz) brown (similar shade) bouclé yarn

4mm (G/6) crochet hook

Sewing thread to match

HAIR

Length of strands for fringe: 17cm (6½in), cut 10–15 strands

Length of strands for centre of head: 38cm (15in), cut 30–35 strands

Length of strands for centre of head: 34cm (13in), cut 25–30 strands

Length of strands for base of head: 26cm (10in), cut 20–25 strands

YOU WILL NEED

PETER DOLL

BODY

70–80g (2–3oz) stuffing wool

Double knit stockinette for back and arms front and back: 56cm wide x 34cm (22in x 13in)

For front only: 16cm wide x 27cm (6in x 10½in) – total piece 72cm (28in) wide and 34cm (13in) long

Sewing thread to match

1m (40in) extra-strong thread for tying the neck

FEATURED NEEDLE FELTED HEAD

35g (1¼oz) lanolin-rich core wool basic shape + 5g (³⁄₁₆oz) added features

Double knit stockinette 23cm x 23cm (9in x 9in)

Chocolate brown and dark red embroidery thread

1m (40in) extra-strong thread

HAIR

15g (½oz) of chestnut brown alpaca top
Sewing thread to match

TOOLS FOR MAKING TOMKE AND PETER

Felting needle (medium #38)

Sewing needle

Long doll's needle

Scissors

Single 6mm (US10) knitting needle or similar for stuffing wool into limbs

1

Head

Make a Featured Needle Felted Head (see p39) for Tomke and Peter.

The finished heads need to be approximately 9cm (3¾in) diameter.

2

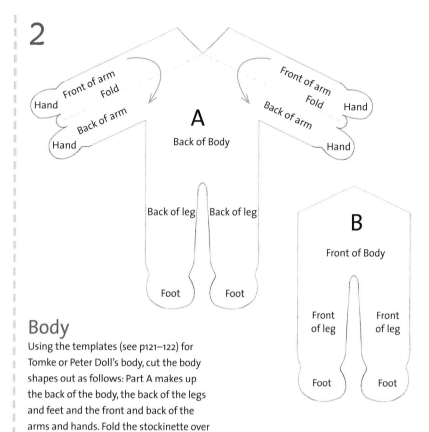

Body

Using the templates (see p121–122) for Tomke or Peter Doll's body, cut the body shapes out as follows: Part A makes up the back of the body, the back of the legs and feet and the front and back of the arms and hands. Fold the stockinette over along the fold line as indicated to make the arms.

Part B makes up the front of the body and the front of the legs and feet.

3

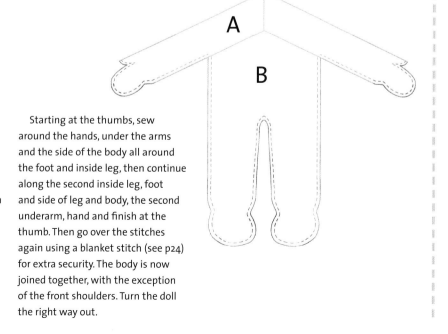

Pin the two parts A and B together inside out. Allowing 5mm (³⁄₁₆in) seam and using a backstitch (see p23) with doubled-up thread, sew the two parts together. Keep the stitches neat and small, pulling the thread tight with each stitch, but not so tight that it pulls the fabric. This part of making up the doll can take the longest but it is definitely worth it to have a secure seam.

Starting at the thumbs, sew around the hands, under the arms and the side of the body all around the foot and inside leg, then continue along the second inside leg, foot and side of leg and body, the second underarm, hand and finish at the thumb. Then go over the stitches again using a blanket stitch (see p24) for extra security. The body is now joined together, with the exception of the front shoulders. Turn the doll the right way out.

4

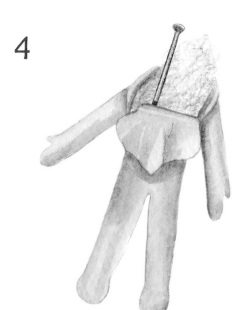 

Next stuff the doll as follows: start by stuffing each foot. I find it useful stuffing the two legs simultaneously. Use a thick knitting needle to get the wool tight into the foot part. Then work your way up the leg always stuffing smaller amounts of wool down with the knitting needle. Leave a small space at the top of the legs so that you can move these later in case the doll needs to sit. These will become the joints.

Roll up an oval shape and fit it inside the body. If this is not big enough, remove it and add more wool. You can also make a smaller oval shape and fit it inside the doll where the bottom is to give it a more distinct shape. This is also the time when you could add a sand pouch (see below) into the doll instead of a wool ball to add weight and stability. Pad the body out where necessary, for example add a little more wool to the tummy area to give the doll a belly.

YOU WILL NEED

Thin stockings or tights 15–20 denier
Sand 250–300g (9–10½oz)

OPTIONAL EXTRA: SAND POUCH

To give the doll a heavier more realistic weight you may choose to use clean dry sand to create a weighted sand pouch that sits inside the doll and to help it sit up.

1. The finer the sand the more times you will have to double-up the stocking. Start by filling the sand into the toe part of the stocking. Then twist the top and fit over the now-filled stocking again. Repeat this process until there is no sandy residue when you pat the pouch.

2. Once you have stuffed the legs of the doll, place the sand pouch into the doll where you imagine his or her bottom to be. Then make the body filling according to the instructions and place in front of the sand pouch. You may have to squeeze the sand and wool into the right place.

5

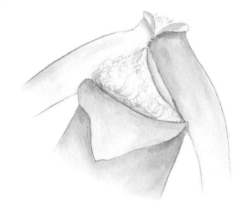 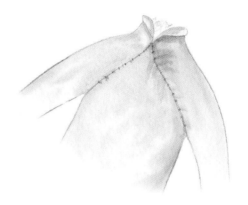

The upper body should be full with the two front shoulder flaps still loose. Stuff the arms as you did with the legs. Using an invisible stitch, sew each front shoulder together (like a raglan sleeve).

The seam will allow the arms to move forward more naturally. Once sewn together you will just end up with the hole in the top for the head. If the body needs bulking out add more wool.

6

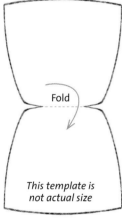

Fold

This template is not actual size

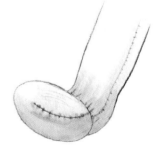

YOU WILL NEED

Skin-coloured stockinette (to match the doll) 5cm x 8cm (2in x 3¼in)
Sewing thread to match
Sewing needle
Small pinch of wool

Feet

You can keep your doll's feet simple in shape (see below) as for Peter doll, or you could add an extra foot / toe part, as was done for Tomke doll, so that your doll can wear shoes.

OPTIONAL EXTRA: FEET

You can give either of these dolls more realistic feet by sewing an addition onto them.

1. Using the template (see p122) cut the stockinette and fold it in half so the wrong side is on the outside. Sew the sides together, shaping it round towards the folded edge.

2. Turn the right way round and fill with a little wool. You need to be able to sew the toe part onto the front of the foot without the stuffing wool getting in the way. Use an invisible stitch and sew the underneath of the toe into the seam, covering the seam and creating a new one. The toe part should stick out at a right angle.

7

Head

Once the body has been stuffed and the front shoulder parts have been sewn together, use your fingers to make an indentation in the wool stuffing at the top into which the fabric ends of the neck of the head can disappear. Pin the head into place or secure it with a few stitches, making sure it is in the right place and position.

Sew the head on with an invisible stitch always going in and out of the doll's body fabric and in and out of the doll's head base, as close to the thread around the neck as possible. Diligent sewing pays off and going round the base of the head three to four times, sewing the two parts together, will keep it secure.

8

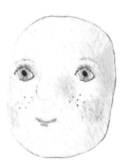

Face

Tomke has a needle felted face, and Peter has a simple embroidered face. You can decide what sort of face to give your doll, see p41 for more ideas.

Tomke has freckles added to her cheeks which were made by using a thin brown felt tip pen. You can rub some blusher into the cheeks, or use a non-oily pink crayon to add a rosy glow to your doll's face.

9

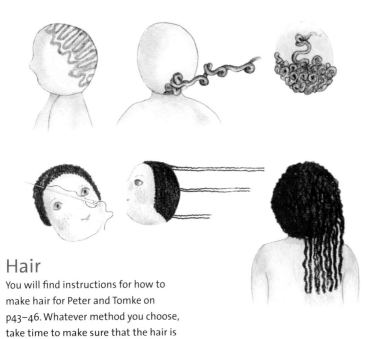

Hair

You will find instructions for how to make hair for Peter and Tomke on p43–46. Whatever method you choose, take time to make sure that the hair is securely attached to the head.

10

Finishing

You can make a dress, trousers, jumper, hat and shoes or slippers for your doll. For ideas see p78-89.

Fenja and Felix Dolls The Stockinette Baby Doll

I always felt that there should be a more baby-shaped doll and decided to make a Waldorf Baby Doll many years ago. I still love the fact that this doll is slightly smaller than the others and you could easily fit a tiny nappy onto him or her as the legs are more U-shaped. I call this doll Fenja, as the real Fenja is my youngest daughter and will always be the baby.

Both dolls are made in the same way but the light-skinned Fenja Doll has hair and a removable hat, whereas Felix, the dark-skinned doll, has a simple sewn-on fringe and a hat that is fastened to the head.

YOU WILL NEED

HEAD
15g (½oz) stuffing wool
Cotton gauze tube 2.5cm x 40cm long (1in x 15¾in)
Stockinette 16cm x 16cm (6in x 6in)
Embroidery thread (or needle felting wool) for eyes and mouth

BODY
44cm x 16cm (17in x 6in) stockinette
Stuffing wool 40–50g (1½–1¾in)

HAIR
Felix Doll: brown embroidery thread
Fenja Doll: bouclé yarn in light yellow/blonde 20g (¾oz)

CLOTHES AND ACCESSORIES
Felt tunic: 20cm x 17cm (7½in x 6½in) wool-viscose felt
Hat: 17cm x 11cm (6½in x 4⅜in) felt or velour
Cord: 2cm x 20cm (¾in x 7½in) (or make your own, see p22)

TOOLS
Sewing needle
Scissors
Crochet hook (for Fenja Doll only)
Long doll's needle

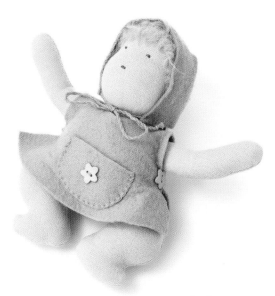

Finished Measurements

21cm (8in) tall

1

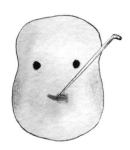

Head

Make a Double Layered Head (see p33). You can embroider or needle felt eyes and a mouth onto the face.

Give your baby rosy cheeks by gently brushing a clean red or pink crayon or blusher onto the face and rubbing it in with your fingers.

2

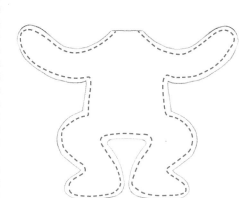

Double up your sewing thread for extra strength if you are sewing by hand. Use a backstitch and keep the stitches neat and small.

The seam allowance is only 5mm (³/₁₆in) wide, so once you have sewn around the body go over the seam again, this time using a blanket stitch (see p24) to prevent the edges fraying and to add strength.

Body

Cut two body shapes from the template (see p123) allowing for a 5mm (³/₁₆in) seam. Pin and sew the two body parts right-sides together with a small, neat backstitch all the way round (about 5mm [³/₁₆in] from the edge) except for the neck opening. This part takes the longest if you do it by hand. You can use a sewing machine, but you will need to use a jersey sewing needle for knits.

Turn the body the right way round and begin stuffing by forming firm sausages out of some of the stuffing wool to stuff the legs and arms. Use a knitting needle or similar to get the wool right down into the feet and hands; just be sure not to pierce the fabric. If you can keep the stuffing of the limbs separate from the rest of the body's stuffing it will allow the limbs to move (see p29).

3

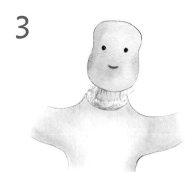
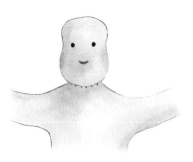

Fitting the head

Stuff the rest of the body, leaving a 'hole' for the loose head ends to fit inside the stuffing wool (so that you don't feel the ends through the stockinette). Make sure that you have stuffed your body nice and firmly. In time the wool will flatten out a bit and if it is stuffed well there won't be any 'flabby' bits in the future.

Insert the loose ends of the head into the body and fasten the head to the neck with a few pins, sew a few stitches and remove the pins. At this stage you must make sure that your head is straight and that it is in the centre of the shoulders. Sew again with small invisible stitches to secure properly. Diligence will pay off when sewing the head on by going around it twice using invisible stitches.

FINISHING TOUCHES

To create a belly button just put a few stitches in where you imagine it would be. You might want to sew a couple of stitches into the groin to bring the legs forward a little and the same with the arms.

4

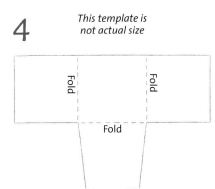

This template is not actual size

Hat and hair

Cut the velour (for Felix) or felt (for Fenja) using the T-shaped hat template (see p125). The stem of the 'T' will be the back of the hat. Fold the three flaps in, right-sides together, to form a three-sided box and sew together where they meet.

Use your thin cord to make a plait or make two lengths that will form the tie for the hat. Sew them into place.

Note that each baby will reflect his/her individuality by being slightly smaller or larger and you might therefore have to adjust the size of (for example) the hat. Your baby will be unique!

5

FELIX DOLL WITH FASTENED HAT

Use the embroidery thread to sew a few strands across the forehead for a fringe, making sure that the ends are well out of sight on top of the head. Then sew the hat to the head with small stitches, going all round the edges of the hat.

FENJA DOLL WITH REMOVABLE HAT

Fit the hat onto the doll and tie it around the chin with a bow.

6

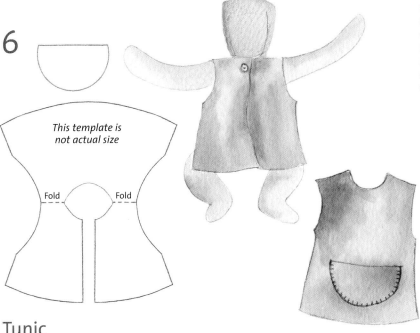

This template is not actual size

Tunic

Cut the felt using the tunic and pocket templates (see p124–125). The tunic is open at the back and needs to be sewn together with a couple of stitches at the sides below the arms (make sure you leave enough room for the arms to move freely).

To allow the back to be opened and closed, cut a small slit into the felt garment to fit one of the buttons and sew this into place. If you are not adding a button, sew a few stitches to close the back, making sure that you leave an opening large enough to fit the head through. Sew a little pocket to the front of the tunic using the embroidery thread (blanket stitch looks nice).

You may add buttons to decorate the tunic but please be aware that they form a hazard for babies and very young children. You could sew on one or two little ties (as with the hat) and fasten the tunic that way at the back.

Dolls' Clothes
and Accessories

Woolly jumper dress

This is a dress that recycles the sleeve of a favourite old sweater or cardigan. Depending on the size of your doll, you may need to use the top of the sleeve, or the bottom where it is usually narrower.

YOU WILL NEED

Single knitted sleeve of a knitted jumper or cardigan
Matching yarn or thread

If you are dressing Tomke Doll (see p67), who is 37cm (14½in) tall, you need the sleeve to be 18cm (7in) wide for the bottom of the dress, 13cm (5in) at the top (the head will need to fit through it) and a total of 18–19cm (7–7¼in) long.

2

Cut arm holes into the sides by laying the dress on top of the doll so you can cut them to measure. They should be no more than 6cm (2¼in) wide. Again, use any of these three options to finish the edges off. If you are crocheting or knitting into the edge, you could make long sleeves for the doll.

1

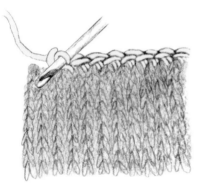

If you have to cut both ends to achieve the measurements required, you will need to 'rescue' the stitches that have been exposed. There are three ways to do this:

1. Pick up the stitches with a knitting needle and knit a couple of rows in a yarn that complements the knitted sleeve.
2. 1dc (US sc) in each stitch, then continue for two rows either in a plain stitch or make a fancier edging by crocheting into each stitch two times with a chain stitch between the double stitches.
3. Hem the edge by folding over and sewing with a running stitch or blanket stitch (you could use knitting yarn for the latter to make a feature of it). You will have to do this at the top and bottom of the dress.

3

Make a cord (see p22), or a crocheted chain from the yarn, then use a large darning needle to thread it through the top edge so you can pull this tighter when the dress is on the doll.

Crocheted dress

This little frock is perfect for the Tomke doll.
Use up any yarn oddments or scraps you have
by changing colour at the end of each round to
make a stripy creation.

YOU WILL NEED
40–50g (1½oz –1¾oz) double knitting yarn
3.5–4mm (E/4–G/6) crochet hook

Finished size: 16cm (6in) across upper body and 24cm
(9¼in) wide across base of dress, 18cm (7in) long
including shoulder loops

Abbreviations:
ch=chain
dc=double crochet (US single)
htr=half-treble (US half-double hdc)
st=stitch
ss=slip stitch

1

Make a chain of 47sts, ss into first chain to form a ring. Htr each
st for 4 rounds, then dc for 3 rounds or until the dress measures
about 6cm (2¼in).

2

1htr in next 3sts, 2 htr in every 4th stitch, repeat to end of round
to increase 11 stitches (total 58sts). Work two rounds in htr. If you
want the dress to be longer than 18cm (7in) including shoulder
straps you need to add more rounds here. Each round of half
trebles extends the length of the dress by about 1.5cm (⁹⁄₁₆in). The
finishing rounds will add another 2cm (¾in).

3

To finish the dress, work two rounds in dc.
Final round: 1dc, 3ch, miss 1st, 1dc. Repeat to the end of the round.

4

To make shoulder straps, lay the dress out with the 'seam' (where
you joined the rounds each time) at the back. Count 4 sts, or
3cm (1¼in) in from the side, join yarn to the top edge, ch 16. Join
the chain at the back, the same distance from the edge on the
other side, with a slip stitch. Work back along the chain in double
crochet (US single). Finish by going into the stitch next to the
chain on the top of the dress.

   Fasten off the yarn and sew in the ends. Repeat on the second
shoulder strap. Sew all the loose yarn ends in and the dress is
finished.

Knitted jumper

The front and back of this slouchy jumper are identical and each part needs 15g (½oz) of yarn, should you decide to make them in different colours as I did. Equally the sleeves need 10g (⅓oz) of yarn each.

YOU WILL NEED

50g (1¾oz) Aran weight cotton (dishcloth cotton)
6mm (US10) knitting needles
Finished size: 20cm (7½in) wide, 14cm (5½in) long from top of the shoulder; Length of sleeves 12cm (4½in). The top should fit either Tomke or Peter Doll.

NOTE
Stocking stitch=knit 1 row, purl 1 row
Garter stitch=knit every row
Cast off (bind off)

1
Front and back
Cast on 26 stitches and knit 4 rows in garter stitch (knit each row). Then change to a stocking stitch (knit one row and purl the next) for 12 rows.

2
Shape for sleeves
Cast off 3 stitches at the beginning of the next 2 rows. You should now have 20 stitches on your needles. Knit another 4 rows in stocking stitch.

3
Shape the neckline
On the next knit row, work 5 stitches, cast off the central 10 stitches, knit to the end of the row. Put the remaining stitches onto a stitch holder (unless you are using a circular needle, then just ignore the first 5 stitches) and work only one side (5 stitches) in a stocking

stitch for another 4 rows, cast off. Rejoin the yarn to the other shoulder and work in stocking stitch for another 4 rows, cast off.

Make another piece the same. With right-sides together sew the shoulders together. Sew the side seams up to the armhole shaping.

4
Sleeves
Cast on 24 stitches and knit 6 rows in stocking stitch. Continue in stocking stitch and cast off 1 stitch at the beginning of the next two rows. Work two rows. Repeat the last four rows a further two times until you have 18 stitches.

Work two more rows in stocking stitch, then the last two rows in reverse stocking stitch, starting with a purl row. Cast off.

Make another sleeve the same way. With right-sides together, fold in half and sew the long edges together. Position the sleeves and sew in place.

Knitted trousers

These little trousers have a drawstring waist to fit your doll comfortably.

YOU WILL NEED
50g (1¾oz) of chunky (bulky) yarn
6mm (US10) knitting needles

NOTE
Stocking stitch=knit 1 row, purl 1 row
Garter stitch=knit every row
Cast off (bind off)

3

Knit both legs simultaneously by dividing your leftover yarn into two, or using both ends of your yarn ball, one part for each leg. To knit both legs simultaneously, knit 22 stitches with the original yarn, then knit the next 22 sts with a new strand of yarn on the same needle. Next row: Knit 22 sts with the new strand of yarn, then knit the next 22 sts with the original yarn, then turn and work the next row in purl. Continue like this for the next 18 rows – depending on how long you would like the legs to be.

4

If you are knitting one leg at a time put 22 sts on a stitch holder, knit the remaining 22 sts back and forth in stocking stitch for 18 rows (make a note of the number of rows). Add 2 rows of reverse stocking stitch (put a purl row on top of a knit row and then purl the next row). Cast off on the third row (purl row). Put the stitches on the holder back onto your needle and knit the same number of rows as before (same length as the other leg) and cast off.

1

Cast on 44 stitches and knit two rows.
Next row: Knit 4, *cast off one stitch, knit 4, repeat from * to the end of the row finishing with 4 knit stitches. Next row: knit each stitch and cast on a new one on top of the ones that had been cast off bringing the total stitches back to 44. This will have made 10 holes which will allow you to add a belt later.

2

Next row: Knit every stitch (44 sts). Continue until you have knitted 14 rows in total (more rows will make the upper body longer).

5

Sew together so that the waist part is sewn up where you imagine a zip or buttons would be. Then sew the two leg parts together with an inside leg seam. Cut a length of yarn approx 1m (40in) long and thread through the eyelets made around the waist and tie in a bow to form a belt and trim the ends.

Peter's dungarees

Dungarees for Peter made from an old jumper are quick and easy to make. Don't worry If your old knitting is a little felted – it will resist fraying.

YOU WILL NEED
An old jumper or knitted garment
Needle and matching thread
2 buttons (optional)

1

Use the template (p122) to cut out the dungarees.

2

With the fabric right sides together, fold the legs into the centre and sew the two inside leg seams together. Sew over the edges to prevent them from fraying. Then sew the two edges above the legs together. This seam will be centre back of the dungarees.

3

Make a hem at the bottom of the legs and sew in place.

4

Neaten the raw edges of the dungaree bib and strap edges if necessary by overstitching or using blanket stitch.

5

Put the dungarees on your doll and stretch the straps over the shoulders. Cut the straps to fit if necessary and either sew the straps in place, or attach buttons to the back, making two button holes in the straps to match.

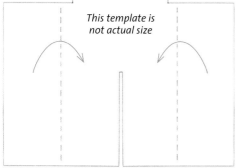

This template is not actual size

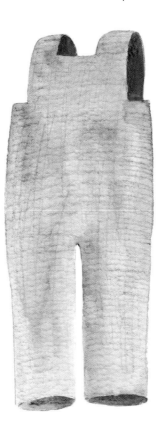

Front of dungarees

Back of dungarees

Crocheted shorts

These shorts are great for Peter Doll or will also work as underwear for a girl version such as the Tomke Doll.

YOU WILL NEED
30g (1oz) of Aran yarn
4mm (G/6) crochet hook

Abbreviations:
ch=chain
dc=double crochet (US sc single)
htr=half-treble (US hdc half-double)
tr=treble crochet (US double)
st=stitch
ss=slip stitch

1

Ch 50 and join into a round. Dc 1 row (US sc) then tr 1 row (US dc). Continue in dc (US single) until the shorts measure about 6cm (2¼in).

2

Start a new round for each leg by splitting the round in half. If you want the shorts to be longer just add more rounds here before you split the legs.

3

For each leg work two rounds of dc (US sc). If you want the legs to be longer just add more rounds here. Finish off the last round as follows: 1dc, 2ch, 1dc, 2ch, repeat, join with ss to first dc to end round, fasten off and sew in ends. Complete the other leg in the same way.

4

Using the same yarn, make a chain of about 55cm (21½in) and tie off. Thread this through the gaps of the treble crochet row (start at the front, miss two, go through one, miss two, go through one etc). This allows you to tie the top of the shorts to stop them from slipping.

Simple knitted hat

Hat knitted in the round

YOU WILL NEED

TO FIT HEAD WITH 8–10cm (3¼–4in) DIAMETER:
100% wool double knitting yarn
4mm (US6) knitting needles

Gauge: 21 stitches over 10cm x 10cm (4in x 4in) in
stocking stitch.

YOU WILL NEED

TO FIT HEAD 10cm (4in) DIAMETER:
50g (1¾oz) 100% wool double knitting yarn
4mm (US6) knitting needles

Gauge: 21 stitches over 10cm x 10cm (4in x 4in) in
stocking stitch.

1

- Cast on 30 stitches
- Knit 6 rows in garter stitch (knit every row)
- Work 37 rows in stocking stitch (alternate knit and purl rows)
- Knit 6 rows in garter stitch, cast off.

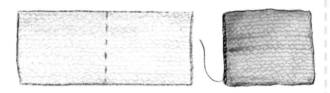

Fold rectangular shape into half and sew two sides together inside
out and then turn right side out.

2

Make a tassel by winding the wool
around two fingers about ten times.

Slip off your fingers and wind the
wool around one end of the loops you
have created, securing the strands of
wool. Cut through the loops on the
other end.

Knot the strand of wool and cut off with about 20cm (7½in)
length remaining (you need this to sew the tassel onto the hat
corner. Make a second tassel the same way. Sew each tassel to the
corners of the hat.

1

Cast on 50 stitches using the circular needle to knit back and
forth in a rib (knit one, purl one) 4 rows.

2

Split stitches into half and start knitting in the round, still
continuing in a rib for another 4 rows (total 8 rows rib).

3

Knit 2sts together every 8th stitch over the next 10 rows until you
have 15sts left.

4

Cut yarn, leaving a 16cm (6in) tail, and knit each st, pulling the
end of the yarn through, gathering all the sts. Pull tight to pull
the top of the hat together and secure by sewing the end in on
the inside of the hat.

5

Sew the gap at the rib part of the hat together. Make a small
pompom if you wish for the top of the hat.

Hat from a sleeve

YOU WILL NEED
Single sleeve from a sweater between 12–15cm (4½–6in)
wide and 18cm (7in) long
Matching yarn or thread

Once the sleeve has been cut off you have two options of how to
close the hat at the top.

1

Turn your sleeve inside out and use a matching knitting yarn to
thread through the top about 2–3 rows down from the exposed
stitches. Gather and secure with a knot, sew in the yarn ends then
cut off. Turn the right way round. Make a small pompom if you
wish for the top of the hat.

2

Turn your sleeve inside out then using a matching yarn or thread
sew the top up so you end up with a rectangle. Turn the right way
round to use as a hat.

TIP
To fit different size heads, have your doll try the
sleeve on, so that the cuff of the sleeve turns
into the band of the hat. This way you can fit
any kind of hat to different dolls and determine
the length of the hat too, in that you cut the
length to fit the doll. Make sure to leave enough
fabric so you can close the hat at the top.

Crocheted slippers

The pattern for these slippers was designed by me many years ago when I made slippers for my own children as babies, toddlers, young children and teenagers. I have adapted it here for you to make little boots for dolls. The great thing about these boots (and the reason why I made them for my children when they were babies in the first place) is that you can tie them tight and therefore hopefully avoid dramas of losing one or both!

YOU WILL NEED

6cm x 12cm (2¼n x 4½in) wool-viscose felt sheet
Embroidery thread and needle
10g (⅓oz) double knitting yarn (more if you are making a cord)
Crochet hook size 2.50mm (USC/2)
3–5mm (⅛–¹⁄₁₆in) or short length of velvet ribbon (or make a cord)

Abbreviations:
ch=chain
dc=double crochet (US sc single)
htr=half-treble (US hdc half-double)
tr=treble crochet (US double)
st=stitch
ss=slip stitch

1

This template is not actual size

Cut out two identical shapes in felt using the template (p125).

2

Blanket stitch around the edge of the felt sole. Space the sts 5mm (³⁄₁₆in) apart and 5mm (³⁄₁₆in) deep – about 22–23sts in total. Keep pulling them tight so that the slipper sole bends inwards slightly (not too tight).

   Tip: you could make a small dot onto the felt base where your blanket stitches go if this helps you to keep the right measurements.

3

Fold into half lengthways and count four blanket stitches from one folded end. Join yarn to the 4th blanket stitch and dc (US single) a whole row.

4

Next row: 1htr in each st (US half-double) (or two rows of dc). You should now have an oblong shape: a base with crocheted sides going up, a little like an open boat.

5

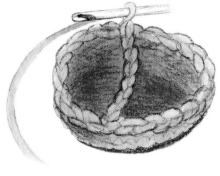

Ch8 across the top of the slipper and ss into the opposite side in the 4th stitch from the folded edge (mirror image of the first 4th stitch). You are going to 'fill' the space between the crochet chain and the tip by crocheting in the round into every other stitch (including the chain) with double crochet stitches. Two rounds will close the gap to create a loafer-shaped slipper. Fasten off.

6

Re-join the yarn to the corner where the top part of the slipper meets the open back, dc into that stitch going all the way round the shaft. This will become the ankle of the slipper and the more rows you add the higher the slipper will become. This part needs to be nice and wide so you may want to try it onto your doll's foot making sure it will slip on easily. Don't worry if it feels too wide as we will add a ribbon or cord to it later to pull it tight so it stays on. Continue in dc for no more than three rows.

7

Next row: 1dc, 2ch, miss a stitch, 1dc into the next st, 2ch, repeat. Next row: dc (US single) into every stitch and then into the chain and so on. This row will take a ribbon or cord to tie the slipper onto the foot of the doll. Add one last row, fasten off and sew in your ends. Make the second slipper in the same way.

8

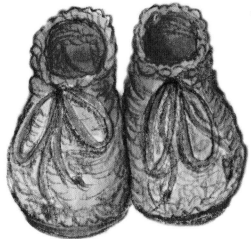

Thread a thin ribbon or cord (see p22), about 3–5mm (1/8in–3/16in) wide, through the shaft of the slippers starting at the front. There should be the right number of loops to end up coming back out again at the front but if not you need to jump one either at the back or front to have the two ends of ribbon coming out side by side at the front in order to tie them.

Dolls' House Dolls
and Accessories

The Dolls' House Family

There is something very charming about being able to create tiny dolls and adding family members, perhaps even matching them individually to a family you know or your own. You may decide to choose the colour of the skin, hair and eyes to give different features to your miniature dolls. I have tried hard in this book to source materials that allow you to make dolls of the world, in different colourful ways. I am also hugely aware that the nuclear family as we have known it for centuries is changing and the dolls you can make here will allow you that flexibility too.

I love using the wool-viscose felt sheets for these dolls as there is no need to hem anything. Cutting the fabric is easy and sewing the felt together with a blanket stitch looks neat. It is also forgiving, as stitches become invisible as they sink into the soft fluff of the felt. Keep any felt off-cuts to use for tiny pockets or other details on the clothing – you never know when they might be useful. As a final note, do not be fooled by the small size of the dolls and assume that they take less time to make! Sewing can be quite fiddly and requires patience and nimble fingers. Adding the details at the end can be fun, but again, very time-consuming.

OPTIONAL EXTRAS
The beauty is in the detail. I love embellishing the dolls' house dolls with miniature decorations and you may find you have some of them already at home – tiny buttons, tiny satin ribbons and flowers, trim and ribbon, lace or fabric with motifs, leather strips or cord and many more. You can add these to the dolls and personalise them to your liking.

Heads

The heads of the Dolls' House Dolls are similarly made to the larger dolls but start out by having a pipe cleaner inside the head to allow them to stand and for adding limbs. I don't distinguish between child and adult heads as they can be similar sizes. If you wish to make children's heads smaller, there is a flexibility of 1–2cm (³/₈–³/₄in) size difference possible. In other words, the cotton gauze will fit comfortably over a 3cm (1¼in) and a 5cm (2in) head. There are two types of heads that you can make:

1.   Featured Head
2.   Featured Needle Felted Head

YOU WILL NEED
1 x 15cm (5³/₄in) extra-strong pipe cleaner
3g (³/₃₂oz) lanolin-rich wool batts in cream (I use organic South German Merino)
15cm (5³/₄in) of 1.5cm (⁹/₁₆in) cotton gauze tube
75cm (29½in) extra-strong thread
6cm x 8cm (2¼in x 3¼in) single-knit stockinette or jersey fabric – grain of fabric running lengthways
Sewing thread to match

1

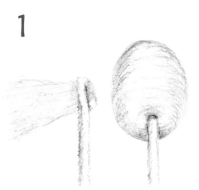

Featured Head

Using your pipe cleaner, begin by wrapping wisps of the wool batt about 2cm (¾in) from the top. Wrap the wool flat like a ribbon so it does not become 'string-like' but stays flat. Then bend the pipe cleaner end over, therefore trapping the wrapped wool. This will make sure that no sharp pipe cleaner wire will be exposed at any time. Continue to wrap the remainder of the wool around the top of the pipe cleaner. Make sure it is a tight wrap and you will find that the wool will 'stick' to itself without popping open. Once the head measures about 3cm–4cm (1¼in–1½in), stop wrapping.

2

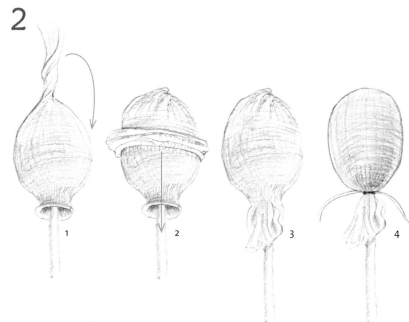

Use your 15cm (5¾in) of cotton gauze and slip the wool head inside one half of the tube length. Twist the tube at the top of the wool ball (1), turn and slip down (2) over the already covered ball to create a second layer (3). You should end up with enough tube ends to pull tight and secure with about 20cm (7½in) of the extra-strong thread (4).

3

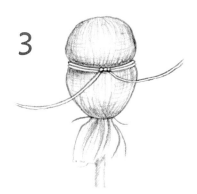

Use 30–35cm (12–14in) of the extra-strong thread to wind around the centre of the head twice, pulling tight to make an indentation, then secure with a double overhand knot (see p24). Imagine that where you tied the knot is where the nose of the doll will be.

4

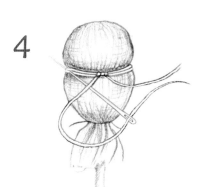

Thread one of the ends of threads onto a needle. Imagine where the ear would be, following the eye line to the side of the head, and sew the thread into the fabric and around the tied thread two or three times to attach the eye line thread onto the side of the head.

5

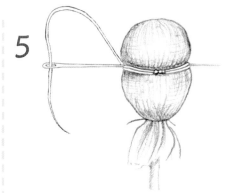

Finish by going all the way through the head, coming out on the other side where the second ear is and securing the thread. Then repeat the process with the other end of the thread, on the other side of the head.

6

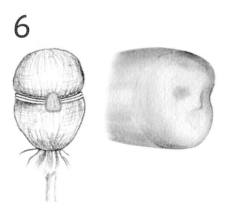

ADDING A NOSE (OPTIONAL)

Roll a tiny amount of wool between your fingers into a ball and sew this onto the top of the eye line knot. To check if the nose is in proportion, stretch the stockinette fabric across the face. This will give you an idea what the finished face will look like. You can change the size of the nose if necessary.

7

Sew the stockinette fabric with a small backstitch along the long side with the colour matching thread, leaving about 5mm (³/₁₆in) seam allowance.

8

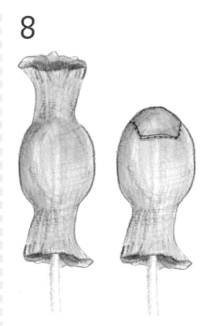

Turn inside out and fit onto the head so that the seam is at the back. Leave about 1–2cm (³/₈–³/₄in) around the neck and fold the remainder of the tube over the back of the head so that there are no creases on the forehead or face. Fasten off and sew the thread to the back of the head.

9

Pull the stockinette down and tie the neck with the remaining length of the extra-strong thread using a double overhand knot (see p24).

ADDING FEATURES: EYES AND MOUTH

If you wish to add eyes and a mouth to the face, you can either needle felt these details on or you can embroider them.

Embroidered face

If you are embroidering, you will need to split the embroidery thread and use just two strands; thread these onto a sewing needle.

Starting with the eye, secure your thread at the back of the head and going through the whole head come out where the first eye should be.

Sew a couple of times using tiny stitches back and forth, then go to the other eye by inserting the needle just below the stockinette fabric. Repeat the stitch for the second eye before coming back out at the back of the head. Secure your thread there.

Repeat this process for the mouth.

Needle felted face

If you are needle felting the details onto the face, you will need a medium or fine felting needle and tiny wisps of coloured wool for the eyes and mouth. Place the wisps of wool into place on top of the stockinette face and stab gently into the fabric so that it leaves a small dot for the eyes and a slightly larger one for the mouth.

You now have a finished head on a pipe cleaner stalk ready to add pipe cleaner arms and legs etc.

1

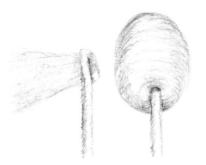

Needle Felted Head

Using your 15cm (5¾in)-long extra-strong pipe cleaner, begin wrapping wisps of the wool batt around the top, about 1cm–2cm (³⁄₈in–¾in) along. Wrap the wool flat like a ribbon so it does not become 'string-like' but stays flat. Then bend the pipe cleaner end over, trapping the wrapped wool. This will make sure that no sharp pipe cleaner wire will be exposed at any time. Continue to wrap the remainder of the wool around the top of the pipe cleaner. Make sure it is a tight wrap and you will find that the wool will 'stick' to itself without popping open.

2

When the head measures 3cm (1¼in) in diameter you can begin to use the medium felting needle to firm-up the shape by stabbing all over. If you are making a smaller child's head skip the next stage and go straight to 'Adding Features' (see p97). If you are making a larger adult head, continue to wrap the wool ball with another few thin but firm layers of wool and felt down again until the head measures approximately 5–6cm (2–2¼in).

3

Once the head is the right size and firmly felted, tear off a short strand of wool and lay this over the forehead of the doll. Felt it down flat at the back first, and on the front of the head felt it down so that it is slightly protruding like an exaggerated forehead. Repeat the same process with the chin.

4

EYES

Now use your felting needle to make two indentations by concentrating your needle in one spot where the eyes are going to go. They need to be positioned half way between top and bottom of the head. The further apart they are, the cuter the face will look.

5

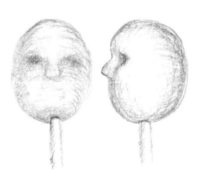

NOSE

Shape a tiny ball of wool by rolling it between your fingers and felt onto the face right between the two eye indentations.

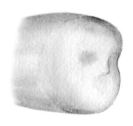

You can check the features and how they will appear by stretching the stockinette fabric over the face. Once you do this the exaggerated features will become less obvious. You can still adjust any of them at this stage.

6

Next take your stockinette fabric and sew together with a neat and small backstitch along the long side with the colour-matching thread. Leave about 5mm (³/₁₆in) to the edge.

7

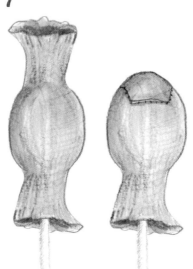

Turn inside out and fit onto the head so that the seam is at the back. Leave about 1–2cm (³/₈–³/₄in) around the neck and fold the remainder of the skin-coloured tube over the back of the head so that there are no creases on the forehead or face. Run the thread to the back of the head with invisible stitching and fasten off.

8

Finally pull the stockinette down and tie the neck with the remaining length of the extra-strong thread using a double overhand knot (see p24).

9

ADDING FEATURES: EYES AND MOUTH

If you wish to add eyes and a mouth to the face, you can either needle felt these details on or you can embroider them.

You now have a finished head on a pipe cleaner stalk ready to add pipe cleaner arms and legs etc.

Doll with short or long top and trousers

These two dolls were made with featured heads with a nose (see p93). Your starting point will be the head on a pipe cleaner stalk. The completed doll body can be made into either a girl or boy. Wooden feet makes them able to stand up easily.

YOU WILL NEED

MATERIALS PER DOLL

2 x 15cm (5¾in) extra-strong pipe cleaners

8cm x 15cm (3¼in x 5¾in) felt sheet in green for the trousers

11cm x 15cm (4⅜in x 5¾in) felt sheet in indigo for the top

5g (³⁄₁₆oz) of lanolin-rich wool batts

Embroidery thread for sewing up the clothes

3cm x 6cm (1¼in x 2¼in) stockinette for hands

2 x wooden shoes (if not available, use an extra 3cm x 6cm (1¼in x 2¼in) piece of stockinette to make two feet, the disadvantage being that the doll will not be able to stand on its own)

Glue (such as PVA, fabric glue or a glue gun)

50cm (20in) extra-strong thread for tying the hands (use more if feet are made in the same way)

1

2

ARMS

Make arms by twisting one pipe cleaner round the top of the pipe cleaner with head attached. Twist the pipe cleaner over the top of the gauze tube and stockinette at the neck. Make sure the arms are of equal length. Don't worry if the arms seem a little wobbly, they will be secured with wraps of wool.

Take a wisp of the wool batts and wrap a thin layer around one end of the arm pipe cleaner. Wrap it flat like a ribbon so it does not twist into a string. Then bend the end in by about 1cm (³/₈in) or more if you are making a small child doll, then cover with more wool so you have a fist

the size of a small pea and the sharp end of the pipe cleaner has disappeared.

Continue wrapping a thin slightly looser cover onto the whole of the arm and wrap around the centre pipe cleaner too. Then make the other hand in the same way.

3

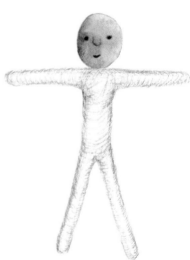

LEGS

Fit the legs by adding the second pipe cleaner onto the central pipe cleaner – about 3cm (1¼in) for a child and 5cm (2in) for an adult – from the head. Use

the central, head pipe cleaner to secure the new length by twisting it around the middle of the leg pipe cleaner upwards and winding it around itself.

Wrap thin layers of the wool round the feet in the same way you did with the hands and use the wool to add bulk to the whole of the figure. As we are custom-making the clothes, you can choose to make a slim or larger build.

4

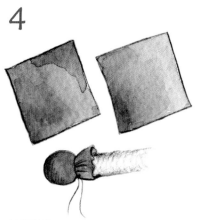

HANDS

Cut the small piece of stockinette in half so you end up with two 3cm x 3cm (1¼in x 1¼in) squares, fit one over the hand and secure with the extra-strong thread using a double overhand knot. Alternatively, you can fit the piece onto the end of the pipe cleaner and using a needle and thread sew tightly around the hand. Cut the excess thread and fabric close to the knot (but not too close!). Repeat on the other hand.

5

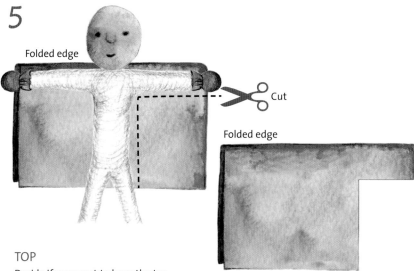

Folded edge

Cut

Folded edge

TOP

Decide if you want to have the top hanging over the trousers (like the girl doll) or the top tucked into the trousers (for the boy doll): start with the item of clothing that will be underneath. With my boy doll the top will be inside the trousers and so I start with the top.

Take the larger piece of felt, fold in half along the short side so that the

fold is at the top. Lay the doll with the arms stretched out on top of the folded felt piece.

Use your scissors and make two cuts: one under the arm and the other along the side of the body. Make sure you leave at least 1cm (³⁄₈in) between the cut edge and the arm/side of the body.

6

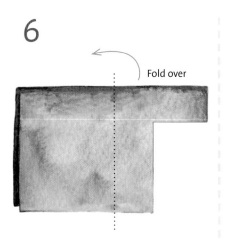

Fold over

Take the felt piece and fold in half so that the first fold stays at the top. You should now have one cut side on top of the uncut side.

7

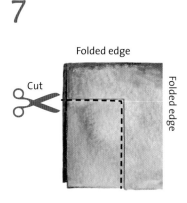

Folded edge

Folded edge

Cut

Use the cut edge as a template and cut in the same way on the other side of the felt to make a symmetrical shape.

8

Keeping the felt folded in half, cut the corner off, which will be a tiny triangular shape out of the folded top corner. When you unfold the sheet this will become a diamond-shaped hole, which will be too small to fit the head through.

9

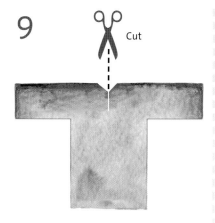

Cut

To fit the head make an incision down the front (or back) of no more than 2cm (¾in). This should be enough now to fit the top onto the doll.

10

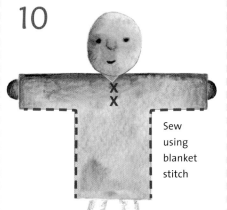

Sew using blanket stitch

Use three strands of coloured embroidery thread and blanket stitch to sew the top together under the arms and along the sides of the body. Lastly, sew up the incision. You can do this in a decorative way, using cross stitches; the opening can be at the front or back.

11

Finally use the skin-coloured thread and sew the hand onto the sleeve ends by using an over stitch (see p23). Repeat on the other side and do the same around the neck, sewing the collar onto the underneath of the head. Finally wrap your thread around the base of the head a few times and pull tight to make the neck more distinct, and then tidy the threads away at the back of the head.

12

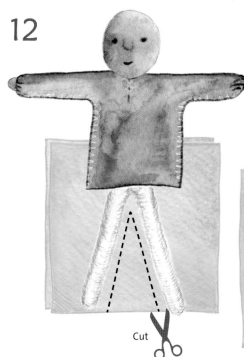

Cut

TROUSERS

Take the smaller piece of felt (trousers) and fold it in half along the short edge and cut there so that you end up with two equal-size pieces approximately 7.5cm x 8cm (3in x 3¼in). Measure these against the doll by holding them onto the lower part of the doll. Cut the two pieces while in place between the doll's pipe cleaner legs. If you need to shorten the trousers, do this too. The trouser legs should be as long as the legs, especially if you are attaching shoes.

Sew along the sides and between the legs using a blanket stitch. Once sewn up, turn inside out, or leave the blanket stitch visible. Slip onto the doll and using a running stitch and coloured embroidery thread, sew around the waist to gather the trousers in. Secure your thread and trousers by going through the doll's body a couple of times from side to side and front to back.

13

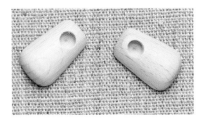

FEET
Use the glue to fasten the feet into the wooden shoes and the hem of the trousers onto the top of the shoes as well, then leave to dry.

14

HAIR
The boy doll has short curly hair made with alpaca or wool tops (see p46) twisted into curls. The girl's hair is made using strands of wool that are sewn on to the head, starting at the back of the neck (see p47) and working up the head in layers.

CLOTHES AND ACCCESSORIES

Satchel

This is just the right bag for any self-respecting doll who is going to work or school. Choose brown for a leathery look.

YOU WILL NEED
8cm x 5cm (3¼in x 2in) wool-viscose felt sheet
Tiny button
Needle and thread

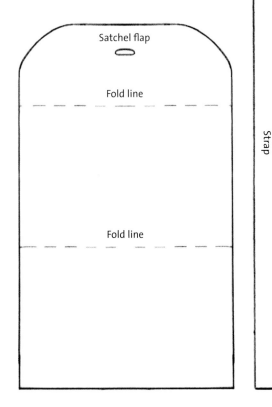

Satchel flap

Fold line

Fold line

Strap

This template is actual size

1

Use the template to cut out one shape in felt.

2

Fold the first two thirds of the rectangle to create the pocket of the bag. Stitch the outside of the seams with blanket stitch (see p24).

3

The rounded edge will become the flap. Fold this over the top of the pocket. Sew on a button to the front of the pocket and make a matching hole in the flap.

4

Cut a strap from the felt sheet approx 8cm (3¼in) long and attach each end to the top corners of the bag.

Waistcoat

This little jerkin will dress a male or female doll.
Add tiny sleeves to make a jacket.

YOU WILL NEED

8cm x 5cm (3¼in x 2in) wool-viscose felt sheet
Tiny button
Needle and thread

1

Use the template to cut out one shape in
felt. Cut two holes for the arms as shown.

2

Fold the top edges back to form lapels
and a collar.

3

Try the waistcoat on your doll to ensure
a good fit. Sew a button on one side and
make a hole on the opposite side.

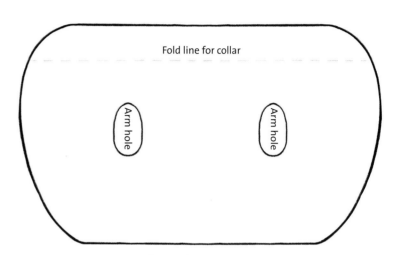

Fold line for collar

Arm hole

Arm hole

This template is actual size

Cap

In the right colour this jaunty cap would suit
any of the dolls.

YOU WILL NEED

8cm x 5cm (3¼in x 2in) wool-viscose felt sheet
Needle and matching thread

1

Use the template to cut out the rectangle shape and peak.

2

Sew the two short edges of the rectangle together.

3

Use your fingers to pinch one open edge of the
rectangle together in a cross shape (see right), then sew the
edges together to create the crown.

4

Attach the small peak at the front edge using overstitch.

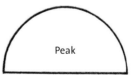

Peak

Head piece

This template is actual size

Doll with dress and apron

This simple doll does not have legs, but the long felt dress with a circular base enables her to stand securely. You can hand-decorate her apron.

Start by making the Featured Head with a nose (see p93).

YOU WILL NEED

MATERIALS PER DOLL:

1 x 15cm (5¾in) extra-strong pipe cleaner

12cm x 22cm (4½in x 8½in) wool-viscose felt sheet

6cm x 6cm (2¼in x 2¼in) wool-viscose felt sheet in the same colour as the dress

9cm x 9cm (3¾in x 3¾in) wool-viscose felt sheet for the apron

Small buttons for the apron (optional)

5g (³⁄₁₆oz) of lanolin-rich wool batts

Embroidery thread for sewing up the clothes

3cm x 6cm (1¼in–2¼in) stockinette to match the face colour (for hands)

50cm (20in) extra-strong thread for tying the hands

1

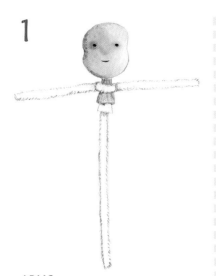

ARMS

Make arms by twisting one pipe cleaner round the top of the pipe cleaner with head attached. Twist the pipe cleaner over the top of the gauze tube and stockinette at the neck. Make sure the arms are of equal length. Don't worry if the arms seem a little wobbly, they will be secured with wraps of wool.

2

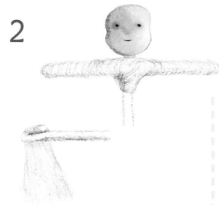

Take a wisp of the wool batts and wrap a thin layer around one end of the arm pipe cleaner. Wrap it flat like a ribbon so it does not twist into a string. Bend the end in by about 1cm (³⁄₈in), then cover with more wool so you have a fist the size of a small pea and the sharp end of the pipe cleaner has disappeared.

Continue wrapping a thin, slightly looser cover onto the whole of the arm and around the centre pipe cleaner too. Make the other arm in the same way.

3

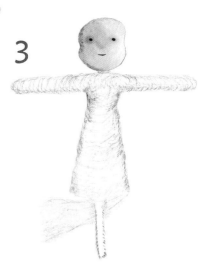

BODY

Wrap more wool batts around the full length of the central pipe cleaner. Aim for a cone shape, with more wool at the base that will help your doll to stand.

4

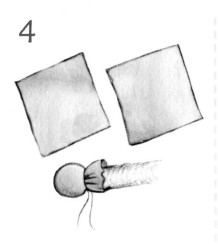

HANDS

Cut the small piece of stockinette in half so you have two 3cm x 3cm (1¼in x 1¼in) squares. Fit one over the hand and secure with the extra-strong thread using a double overhand knot (see p24). Alternatively, fit the piece onto the end of the pipe cleaner and sew tightly around the hand. Cut the excess thread and fabric close to the knot. Repeat on the other hand.

5

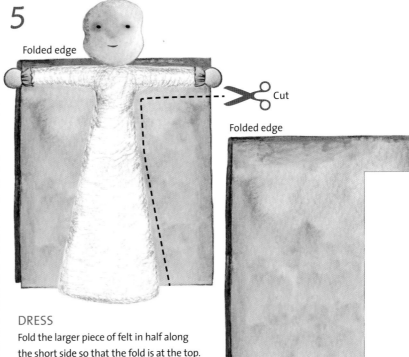

Folded edge

Cut

Folded edge

DRESS

Fold the larger piece of felt in half along the short side so that the fold is at the top. Lay the doll with the arms stretched out on top of the folded felt piece.

Use your scissors and make two cuts: one under the arm and the other along

the side of the body. Make sure you leave at least 1cm (³⁄₈in) between the cut edge and the arm/side of the body.

6–9

COMPLETING CUTTING OUT THE DRESS

Follow the instructions for steps 6–9 of 'Doll with short or long top and trousers (see p100–101) to complete cutting out the dress ready for sewing.

10

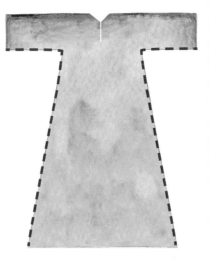

Using two or three strands of embroidery thread, begin sewing the dress using a blanket stitch while on the doll, starting at one side from the bottom to the under arm.

11

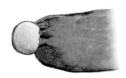

Use a running stitch to go around the edge of the sleeve and pull tight to gather so it fits snugly around the hand. If you prefer the sleeves to be more fitted, you can cut them closer to the arms before sewing them up. You may have to gather the end in. Then repeat this for the other sleeve.

12

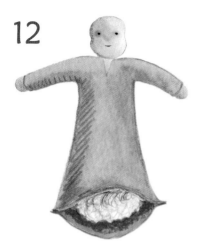

Your doll is now dressed with the base of the dress still open (and the front or back incision still open too).

Decide on the height of your doll and adjust the pipe cleaner inside accordingly. If the dress is too long, this can be folded in, before sewing a base onto the doll. Once you have the right height, stuff more wool inside the dress, but not too much as the doll will stand up better with a flat base rather than one that is bulging.

13

Use the 6cm x 6cm (2¼in x 2¼in) felt square and cut into a disc shape. The shape needs to be about 1cm (³⁄₈in) larger than the base of the dress. Attach the felt disc to the base of the dress and close up using a blanket stitch.

14

FINISHING THE BODY

Sew up the incision at the top of the dress. You can either sew this with an invisible stitch and ordinary sewing thread or make it a feature by using the embroidery thread and making decorative cross stitches.

Use the skin-coloured thread to attach the head to the top of the dress using an invisible stitch. Once you have sewn around the base of the head, wind the thread a couple of times around the head and pull tight. Then secure at the back of the head.

Use the skin-coloured thread and an over stitch to secure each hand to the end of the dress sleeve.

15

APRON

Cut the apron out using the template (see right).

You can leave the apron blank or add a pattern or decoration using thin-tipped coloured felt-tip pens.

Attach the apron to the doll's dress by using small stitches at the top corners on the front of the apron. You may also like to add small buttons here.

You can attach the apron at the back of the body either by more small stitches, or you could add two lengths of cord or embroidery thread to tie into a bow at the back.

This template is actual size

16

HAIR

Using mohair or bouclé yarn, make a small crocheted cap (see p43) and sew securely to the head. Then crochet a simple chain of approximately 15cm (5¾in) long. Attach one end to the back of the head and then wrap round and round to make a bun. Sew in place. You can make a fringe by carpet knotting several strands to the front of the head.

Doll with top and skirt

Start by making the Featured Head with a nose (see p93).

YOU WILL NEED

MATERIALS PER DOLL, ADULT OR CHILD:

1 x 15cm (5¾in) extra-strong pipe cleaner

8cm x 15cm (3¼in x 5¾in) wool-viscose felt sheet in colour of your choice for the skirt (I used pale pink)

6cm x 6cm (2¼in x 2¼in) wool-viscose felt sheet in the same colour as the skirt

11cm x 15cm (4⅜in x 5¾in) wool-viscose felt sheet in colour of your choice for the top (I used mint green)

5g (³⁄₁₆oz) of lanolin-rich wool batts

Embroidery thread for sewing up the clothes

3cm x 6cm (1¼in x 2¼in) stockinette to match the face colour (for hands)

50cm (20in) extra-strong thread for tying the hands

1–2

ARMS
Make the arms following the instructions for the 'Doll with Dress and Apron' (see p104).

3

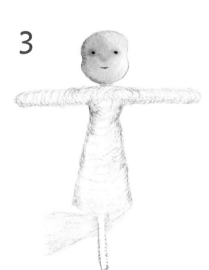

BODY
Wrap more wool batts around the full length of the central pipe cleaner.

4

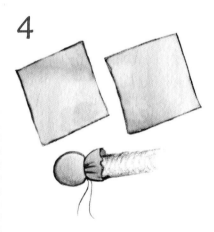

HANDS
Cut the small piece of stockinette in half so you have two 3cm x 3cm (1¼in x 1¼in) squares. Fit one over the hand and secure with the extra-strong thread using a double overhand knot (see p24). Alternatively, fit the piece onto the end of the pipe cleaner and sew tightly around the hand. Cut the excess thread and fabric close to the knot. Repeat on the other hand.

5

Decide if you have the top hanging over the skirt or the top tucked into the skirt. Start with the item of clothing that will be underneath the other. With my doll, the top will be on top of the skirt and so I start with the skirt.

SKIRT
Fold the smaller piece of felt (skirt) in half along the short edge. Cut on the fold to make two equal-size pieces, approximately 7.5cm x 8cm (3in x 3¼in). Measure these against the doll by holding them onto the lower part of the doll. Shorten the skirt if needed.
Sew the two pieces together with an embroidery thread and a blanket stitch along the sides, leaving the top and bottom open.

6

You can add a pattern or design to the skirt material, by drawing your designs on to the felt with thin-tipped coloured felt pens.

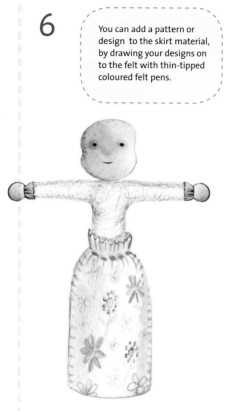

Slip onto the doll and use a running stitch and embroidery thread to sew around the waist to gather the skirt in. Secure your thread and skirt by going through the doll's body a couple of times from side to side and front to back.

7

Decide on the height of your doll and adjust the pipe cleaner inside accordingly. Once you have the right height, stuff more wool inside the skirt but not too much as the doll will stand better with a flat base.

Use the 6cm x 6cm (2¼in x 2¼in) felt square and cut it into a disc shape. The shape needs to be about 1cm (³⁄₈in) larger than the base of the dress. Attach the felt disc to the base of the dress and close up using a blanket stitch.

8

TOP
Take the larger piece of felt, fold in half along the short side so that the fold is at the top. Lay the doll with the arms stretched out on top of the folded felt piece.

Use your scissors and make two cuts: one under the arm and the other along the side of the body. Make sure you leave at least 1cm (³⁄₈in) between the cut edge and the arm/side of the body.

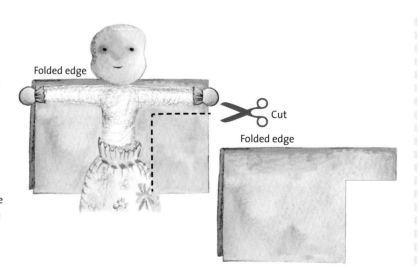

Folded edge

Cut

Folded edge

9

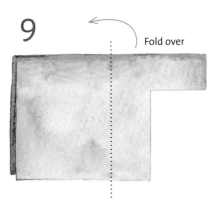

Fold over

Take the felt piece and fold it in half so that the first fold stays at the top. You should now have one cut side on top of the uncut side.

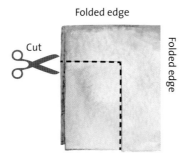

Folded edge

Folded edge

Cut

Use the cut edge as a template and cut in the same way on the other side of the felt to make a symmetrical shape.

10

Keeping the felt folded in half, cut the corner off, which will be a tiny triangular shape out of the folded top corner. When you unfold the sheet this will become a diamond-shaped hole, which will be too small to fit the head through.

11

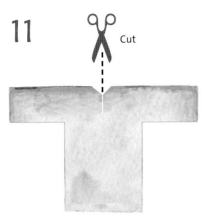

Cut

To fit the head, make an incision down the front (or back) of no more than 2cm (¾in). This should be enough now to fit the top onto the doll.

12

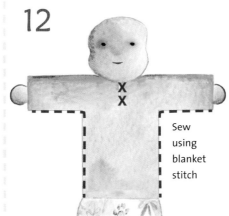

Sew using blanket stitch

Use three strands of coloured embroidery thread and blanket stitch to sew the top together under the arms and side of the body. Lastly sew up the incision. You can do this in a decorative way, using cross stitches.

13

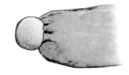

Use the skin-coloured thread and sew the hand onto the sleeve ends by using an over stitch (see p23). Repeat on the other side and do the same around the neck, sewing the collar onto the underneath of the head.

Finally wrap your thread around the base of the head a few times and pull tight to make the neck more distinct, and then tidy the threads away at the back of the head.

14

HAIR

Use dyed sheep locks (Teeswater or similar long curls of wool) and folding each strand in half, sew them on to the head, starting at the back of the neck (see p47) and working up the head in layers.

Baby in cradle

YOU WILL NEED

HEAD
1g (¹⁄₃₂oz) of core stuffing for head
Extra-strong thread
4.5cm x 6cm (1¾in x 2¼in) skin-coloured single-knit stockinette
Sewing thread to match

BODY
8cm x 10cm (3¼in x 4in) wool-viscose felt sheet
5cm x 6cm (2in x 2¼in) of same felt for hat
10cm (4in) length of pipe cleaner
1g (¹⁄₃₂oz) stuffing core wool

CRADLE
10g (¹⁄₃oz) of cotton DK yarn or Aran Merino yarn
3.5mm (E/4) crochet hook

1

BABY

HEAD

Roll the wool for the head into a tight little ball of about 2cm (¾in) diameter by winding it in from one end to the other teasing the fibres out as you go. If it is tight enough it should hold tight while you add the extra strong thread around the centre for the eye line.

Tie the thread around twice and secure with a knot, making sure that you have pulled the thread tight enough to make an indentation. Tie with a double overhand knot (see p24).

2

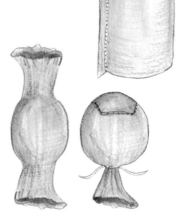

Sew the stockinette into a tube, making sure that the knit runs along the long side, so the stretch is sideways (see p16). Sew using a tiny backstitch allowing 5mm (³⁄₁₆in) for the seam allowance. Turn the right way round and slip over the bound head. Tie the base closed with the extra-strong thread and sew the top closed at the back, away from the face and forehead.

3

Next, split the embroidery thread and thread a single strand onto your needle. Starting at the back of the head where the seam is, insert the needle from back to front to sew a small slit for one eye. Return to the back of the head and repeat for the second eye. Then change colour and make a single stitch for the mouth.

4

Use the hair-coloured embroidery thread (no need to split) and sew a few strands from the top of the head reaching onto the forehead. The hat will cover half of them so make sure that a few neat strands are exposed. It works well if these are of different lengths.

5

Take a wisp of wool batt and wrap a thin layer around one end of the pipe cleaner. Wrap it flat like a ribbon so it does not twist into a string. Then bend the end in by about 1cm (³/₈in) and cover with more wool so you have a tiny fist and the sharp end of the pipe cleaner is encased. Make another fist at the other end of the pipe cleaner.

6

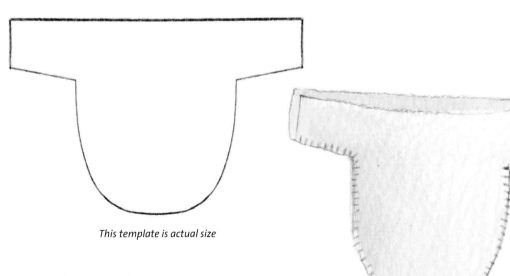

This template is actual size

Using the body template (above) cut two identical shapes from your felt sheet and sew together using a matching thread (a single strand of an embroidery thread works well).

Use blanket stitch (see p24) to sew around both parts, leaving the top open for the head. You can sew this the right way round as the blanket stitch is decorative.

7

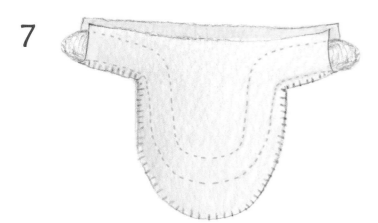

Bend the pipe cleaner with the two fists at each end in half so the two arms are of equal length and fit into the arms of the sewn body. You can bend any excess length of pipe cleaner to sit inside the rounded lower body part of the shape (see above).

Close up the top of the arms using blanket stitch as before, and leaving a gap for the head.

Using an invisible stitch, sew the sleeves onto the wool fists going all the way through the hand a couple of times.

8

Fit the head into the opening at the top of the body and attach with neat overstitches going round two or three times to make sure the head is secure.

9

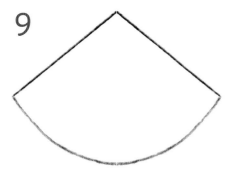

This template is actual size

Finally, cut out a felt hat using the template (left) and sew the straight sides together with the same single embroidery thread you used for the body. Fit onto the head and attach with over stitch.

Make sure the seam of the hat is at the back and the hat reaches all the way down into the neck touching the body.

. . . .

CRADLE

(Abbreviations: ch=chain; dc=double crochet (US treble); st=stitch; ss=slip stitch)

Foundation ring: 3ch.
1st round: 5dc into the first ch.
2nd round: 1dc in each of 6sts.
3rd round: 2dc into each st.
4th round: *2dc in first st, 1dc in next st, rep from*.
5th round: Repeat 4th round.
6th round: Repeat last two rows once more to complete the base.

The next 2–3 rounds: 1dc in each stitch (the sides will curve in). Fasten off and sew in ends.

Stretch with your hands into an oblong basket shape.

Making Handles

Join the yarn to the middle of one side of the basket, 10ch, skip 2sts, join to the same side of the basket with a slip stitch. Repeat for the second handle on the opposite side.

Cover (optional)

Join yarn into the stitch next to the handle, 7ch, ss to the opposite side.
Next: Work double crochet in the round along half the sides of the basket and back across the 7ch.
1st round: 1dc in every other stitch.
2nd round: 1dc in each stitch.
3rd round: 1dc in every other stitch to close the gap.
Fasten off, and sew in ends to finish.

Dolls' house pets

YOU WILL NEED

FOR EACH DOG OR CAT:

10cm (4in) extra-strong pipe cleaner

3g (³/₃₂oz) of main colour wool batts (white, cream or light brown)

Wisps of wool batts in flesh pink, black, beige for details

Medium and fine felting needles #38 and #40

Felting mat

1

CAT AND DOG

Choose your main colour and take a small wispy strand. Wrap the wool around one end of the pipe cleaner to get started. Cover the end with a thin layer and bend the end in by about 5mm (³/₁₆in) to hide the sharp end.

Do this at both ends. When wrapping wool around the pipe cleaner it is important to keep the wool flat like a ribbon and wrap it tightly. This way the wool should just stick to itself.

TIP

The size of the animal can be manipulated by bending the pipe cleaner in more or less at the beginning when covering with the first layer of wool.

2

Build the wool layers up slowly by wrapping more wool but leave a length thinly wrapped for the tail. You may want a really short tail or a long one, depending on whether you are making a cat or dog or what type of dog. The tail of the cat should be at least one third of the length of the body.

3

FINISHING CAT

Build the layers of wool around the body to be about 2–3cm (³⁄₈–1¼in) thick. The head will be slightly smaller at about 2cm (¾in) thick. It helps bending the pipe cleaner in to show the curled shape of the cat. Using your medium felting needle, start by felting the body down gently (try not to stab into the wire as this may break your needle).

4

Make a distinct dent between your cat's body and the head (neck). Felt the base down, so the cat lies flat. Add more wool to keep it in proportion.

5

EARS

Tease two parts of the wool out from the top of the head and felt with the finer needle into two cat ears. As the cat is so small the ears can be wispy. You can position the cat on your felting mat so that you can just stab into the ears to shape a little more. Add a tiny bit of flesh pink wool into the ears.

6

TAIL

The tail of the cat will be underneath the chin, so felt the tail onto the underneath of the head (but mind the wire).

7

EYES AND NOSE

Add tiny black details for eyes and a tiny pink nose.

8

FUR

If you wish, you can add surface colour to give the cat a pattern. Go easy on adding colours as the cat is so tiny that just a couple of patches will be enough.

9

FINISHING DOG

Build the layers of wool around the body to be about 3–4cm (1¼–1½in) thick. The head will be slightly smaller at about 2–3cm (³⁄₈–1¼in) thick. You can make a curled-up dog or a straight one. If you are making a curled-up sleeping dog, bend the pipe cleaner into a curled shape. Using your medium felting needle, start by felting the body down gently.

10

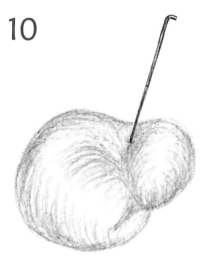

Make a distinct dent between your dog's body and the head (neck). Also felt the base down flat so the dog lies flat. Add more wool to keep it in proportion.

11

EARS

For the ears, take two tiny pinches of the main wool and felt flat on your mat. Make two long round ears or two pointy ears – use your fine needle for the shaping. Then attach to the side of the head by stabbing into the ear and head. This way you can decide whether the ears are hanging flat by the side, or standing up if they are short pointy ears.

> ### COLLAR
> Add a thin strip of coloured wool to make a collar for your cat or dog.

12

EYES AND NOSE

Next add a tiny bit of black for the sleeping eyes (a thin line) and black onto the pointy nose.

13

FUR

Colour your dog in if you wish by adding tiny amounts of different coloured wool either as a dusting or a patch.

14

PAWS

You can make paws in the same way as you made the ears, but do not felt them down so flat and keep them round. Attach in the same way as ears.

Sewing Templates

Here are the templates you will need to make the dolls and accessories in the book. Some of the templates are actual, or full-size, so you can simply trace them onto paper to make a pattern to pin to your material and then cut out.

Most templates have been reduced in size to fit the page, so they will need enlarging to their full size. The easiest way to make your full-size pattern is to trace or photocopy the template, and then enlarge it using a photocopier.

Romi Doll *page 51*

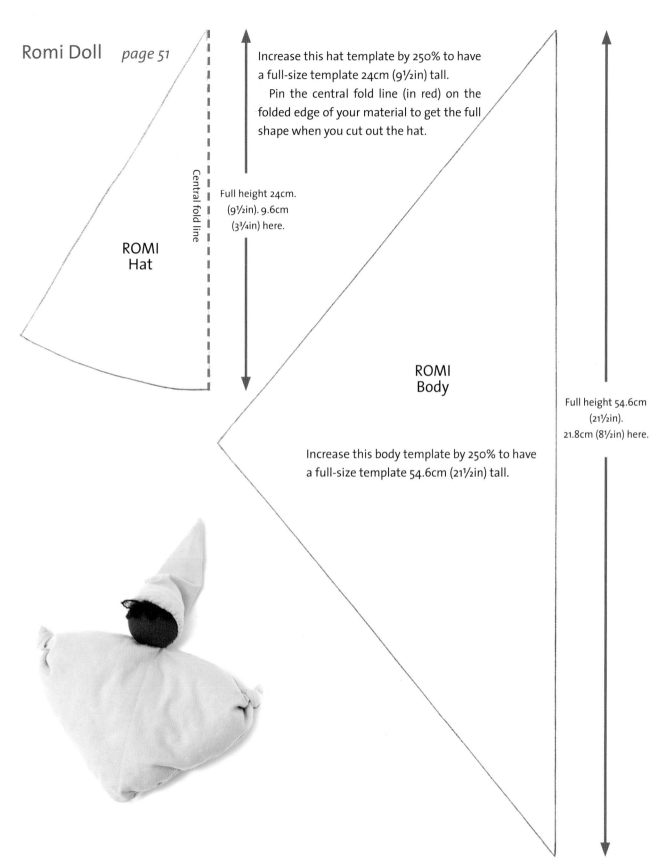

Increase this hat template by 250% to have a full-size template 24cm (9½in) tall.

Pin the central fold line (in red) on the folded edge of your material to get the full shape when you cut out the hat.

Central fold line

Full height 24cm. (9½in). 9.6cm (3¾in) here.

ROMI Hat

ROMI Body

Full height 54.6cm (21½in). 21.8cm (8½in) here.

Increase this body template by 250% to have a full-size template 54.6cm (21½in) tall.

Hannes and Hannah Doll *page 61*

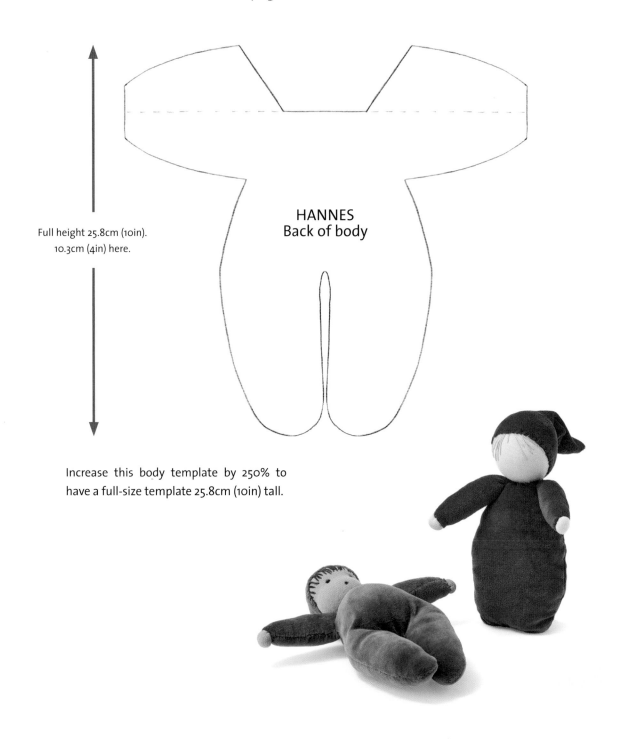

Full height 25.8cm (10in).
10.3cm (4in) here.

HANNES
Back of body

Increase this body template by 250% to
have a full-size template 25.8cm (10in) tall.

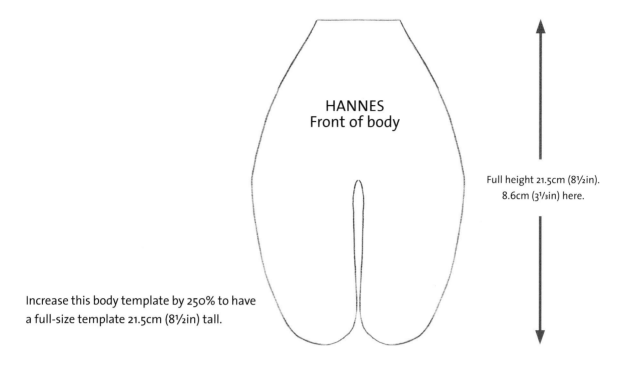

HANNES
Front of body

Full height 21.5cm (8½in).
8.6cm (3⅓in) here.

Increase this body template by 250% to have
a full-size template 21.5cm (8½in) tall.

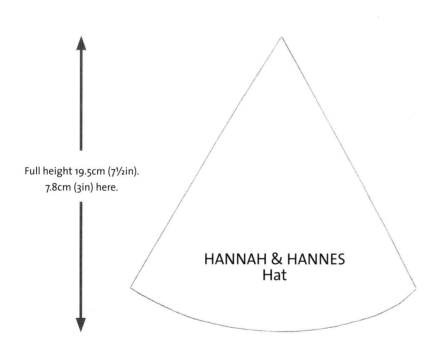

Full height 19.5cm (7½in).
7.8cm (3in) here.

HANNAH & HANNES
Hat

Increase this hat template by 250% to have a
full-size template 19.5cm (7½in) tall.

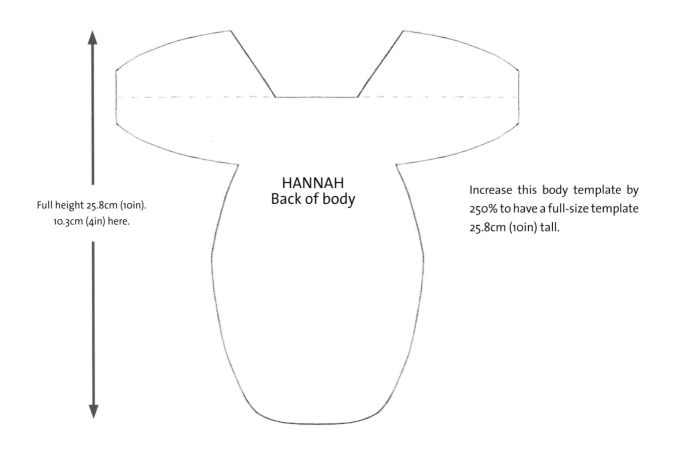

Full height 25.8cm (10in).
10.3cm (4in) here.

HANNAH
Back of body

Increase this body template by 250% to have a full-size template 25.8cm (10in) tall.

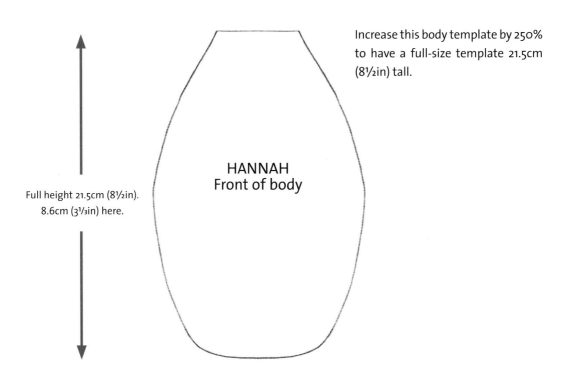

Increase this body template by 250% to have a full-size template 21.5cm (8½in) tall.

HANNAH
Front of body

Full height 21.5cm (8½in).
8.6cm (3⅓in) here.

Tomke and Peter Doll   *page 67*

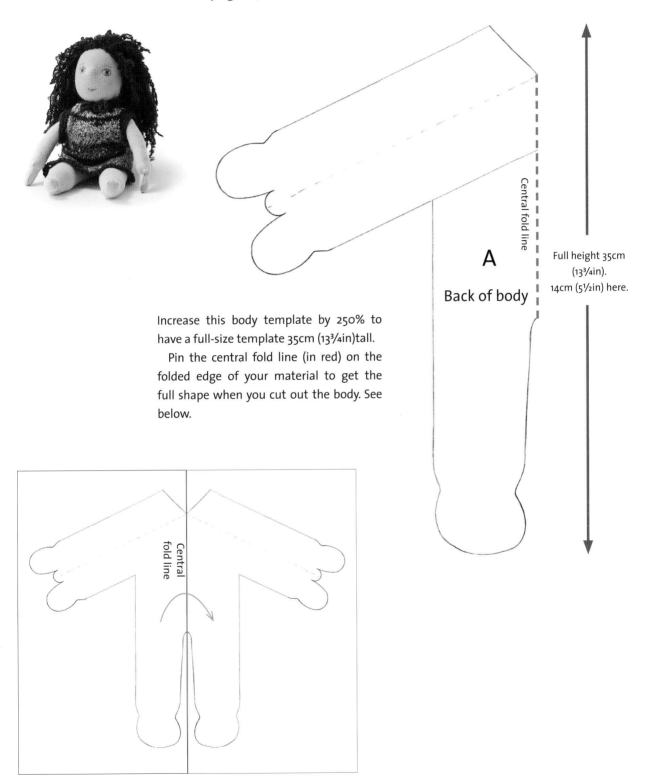

Central fold line

A

Back of body

Full height 35cm
(13¾in).
14cm (5½in) here.

Increase this body template by 250% to have a full-size template 35cm (13¾in)tall.

Pin the central fold line (in red) on the folded edge of your material to get the full shape when you cut out the body. See below.

Central
fold line

Tomke and Peter Doll   *page 67*

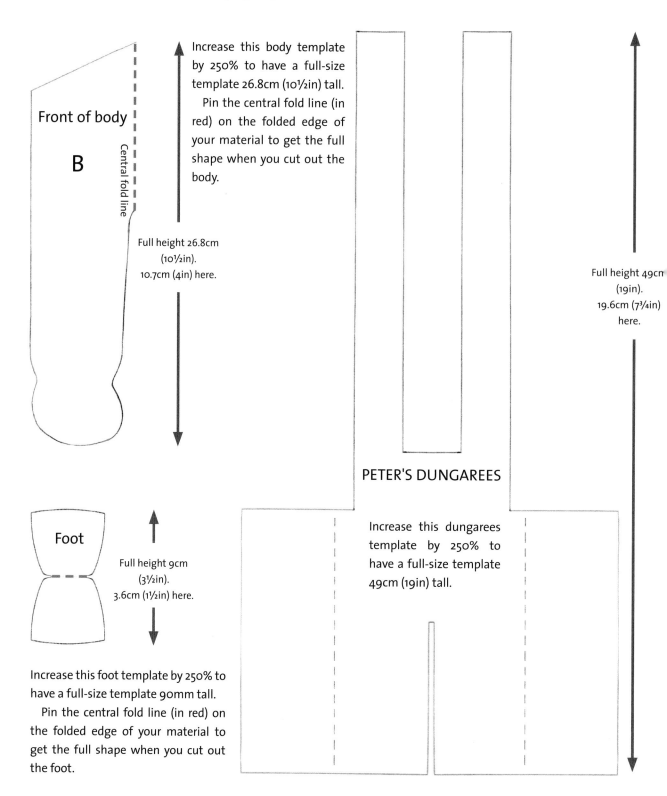

Front of body

B

Central fold line

Increase this body template by 250% to have a full-size template 26.8cm (10½in) tall.

Pin the central fold line (in red) on the folded edge of your material to get the full shape when you cut out the body.

Full height 26.8cm (10½in).
10.7cm (4in) here.

Full height 49cm (19in).
19.6cm (7¾in) here.

PETER'S DUNGAREES

Increase this dungarees template by 250% to have a full-size template 49cm (19in) tall.

Foot

Full height 9cm (3½in).
3.6cm (1½in) here.

Increase this foot template by 250% to have a full-size template 90mm tall.

Pin the central fold line (in red) on the folded edge of your material to get the full shape when you cut out the foot.

Fenja and Felix Doll *page 75*

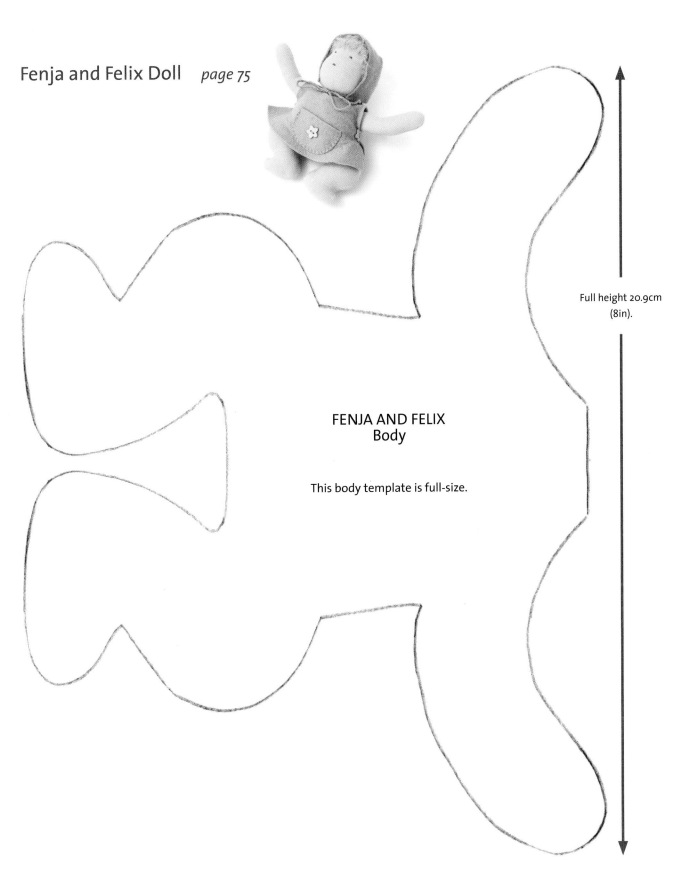

FENJA AND FELIX
Body

This body template is full-size.

Full height 20.9cm
(8in).

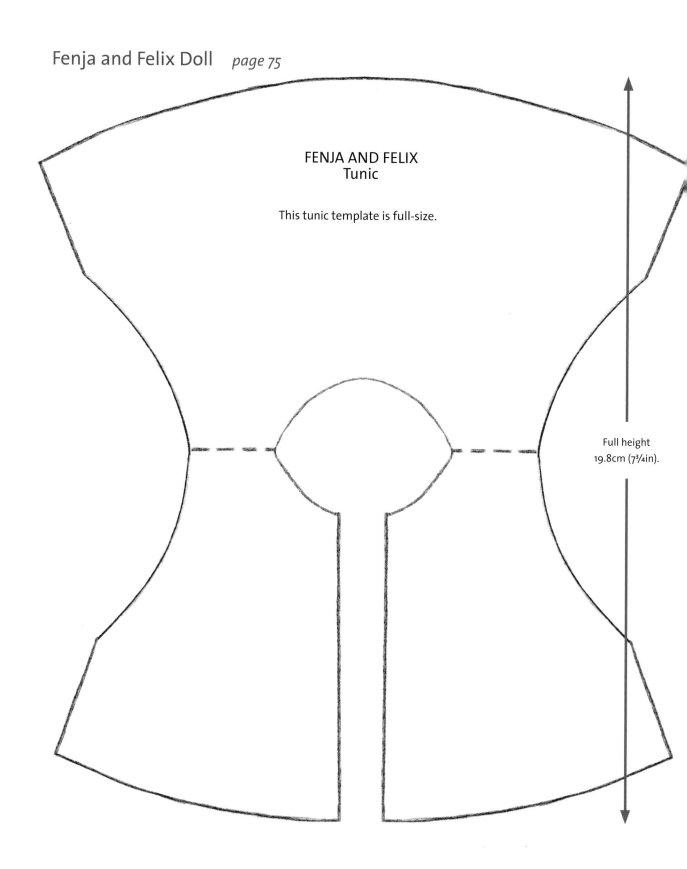

FENJA AND FELIX
Tunic

This tunic template is full-size.

Full height
19.8cm (7¾in).

Full height
4cm (1½in).

FENJA AND FELIX
Tunic Pocket

This pocket template is full-size.

FENJA AND FELIX
Hat

This hat template is full-size.

Full height
11.2cm (4½in).

Crocheted slippers   *page 88*

Full height
5cm (2in).

Crocheted slipper base

This slipper template is full-size.

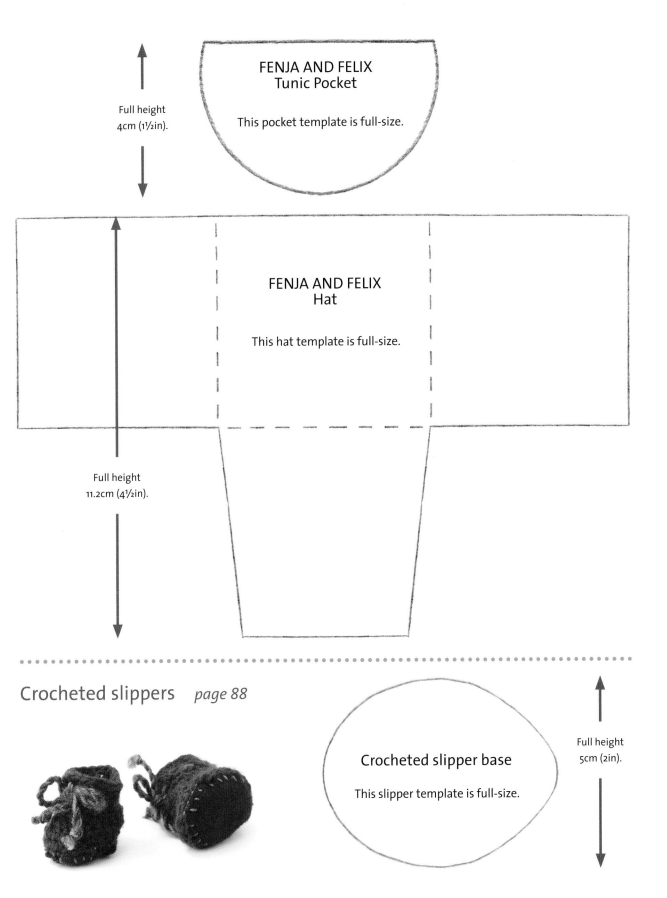

Frequently Asked Questions

HOW DO I CARE FOR MY DOLLS?

It is best to wipe any marks off with a damp cloth using a very mild detergent. Do not put them in the washing machine or wash them in their entirety in a wash basin. As you will have used wool for stuffing and/or hair it is likely to get felted. The dolls become more charming the more loved they look!

TOY SAFETY CERTIFICATION

If you are planning to make dolls as toys to sell for profit you will find that getting a toy safety certificate can be elaborate and expensive. You will need each component in the doll to have the manufacturers' safety certificate (CE) and the materials must be new, not used or recycled. You will have to have your doll tested and then any subsequent dolls you make have to be made in exactly the same way with the same components. As you will see, it is a very complicated and quite restricting process. If you are still planning to sell your dolls without the Toy Safety Certification you have to make it clear that they are not a toy and for display purposes only.

MOTH PREVENTION

Clothes moths love dark and hidden-away spaces, so if your doll gets played with or handled regularly you should not have anything to worry about. If you have to store the doll, put it in an airtight bag or box and add some lavender or cedar balls, which are natural moth deterrents. Using chemicals may not be safe for a child's toy. If you have moths in the doll, you can kill the larvae effectively by putting the doll inside a freezer. This may not kill the eggs but you could repeat the process again later.

CAN I DRAW FEATURES ONTO THE DOLL'S FACE?

In principle yes, but choose your pens carefully. Felt tip pens are less suitable as the ink may run and smudge. Colour pencils or crayons are a better option. Crayons work particularly well for blushing cheeks and pencils for adding freckles.

CAN I USE TOY STUFFING?

Yes, you can use ordinary toy stuffing from any proprietary brand.

CAN I MAKE A VEGAN DOLL?

Yes, you can! Use synthetic toy stuffing and either plant-based fibres for hair such as bamboo and cotton or synthetic yarn. The doll's clothes / accessories can be made from alternative materials too.

Resources

England

THE MAKERSS
www.themakerss.co.uk
info@themakerss.co.uk

For all supplies used in this book and needle felting kits, materials, accessories, tools, tutorials, workshops and talks.

The Makerss
Unit 19
Nailsworth Mills Estate,
Nailsworth, GL6 0BS
Tel 01453 839454

Facebook:
www.facebook.com/themakerss.co.uk
and
www.facebook.com/everyoneamaker

Twitter: **@themakerss**
Instagram: **@themakerss**

Australia

MORNING STAR CRAFTS
Tel: +61 (03) 5985 6797
www.morningstarcrafts.com.au

WINTERWOOD TOYS
9 Colman Road
Warranwood
Victoria 3134
Tel: +61 (03) 9879 0426
www.winterwoodtoys.com

Canada

BEAR DANCE CRAFTS
Tel: +1 (250) 353 2220
www.beardancecrafts.com

MAPLEROSE
265 Baker Street
Nelson BC
V1L 4H4
Tel: +1 (250) 352 5729
www.maplerose.ca

USA

A CHILD'S DREAM COME TRUE
214-A Cedar Street
Sandpoint
Idaho 83864
Tel: +1 (208) 255 1664
www.achildsdream.com
info@achildsdream.com

PARADISE FIBERS
225 W. Indiana
Spokane, WA 99205
Tel; +1 (509) 536 7746
www.paradisefibers.com

Acknowledgements

My biggest thanks as always has to be to my family – herewith as a means of an apology for my absentmindedness, weekends and holidays spent making and writing and compromising on precious family time and wholesome home-cooked meals. I will not even mention my bad moods. Thank you to my children for letting me use their names for the dolls and thank you to my husband Simon who has stood alongside me, so I could fulfill this part of myself.

A big thank you must go to my business partner and beautiful human being Sophie Buckley who has supported and encouraged me to write this book. I know it came at a cost.

Next I would like to thank Katy Bevan, my editor who has kept me on track, provided me with the much -needed book plan and 'big picture' and who has been hugely sensitive to the nature of the book. Thank you too, Lucy Guenot for your usual excellent quality of drawings and design. You bring the book to life for me.

Thanks also to Ollie Perrott for his lovely photos of dolls, people, hands and accessories. The images are the icing on the cake. Thank you to Sarah, Indira and Elijah May-Pilcher for being such agreeable models.

I also want to express my deep gratitude to Martin Large, without whom this book (nor my previous two) wouldn't exist. You finally got your doll book!

Steffi

More books from Hawthorn Press

Making Needle Felted Animals

Over 20 wild, domestic and imaginary creatures
Steffi Stern, Sophie Buckley

Making Needle Felted Animals is an essential guide for anyone interested in the popular craft of needle felting. Whether you are completely new to needle felting or an experienced felter, this book will have something to offer, from precise instruction to creative inspiration.

Written by two authors expert in making and teaching crafts to students of all ages and abilities, instructions are easy to follow and include practical yet creative ideas to fix common mistakes. The projects arise from a genuine love of the natural world and animals, whether they be family pets or wild creatures.

'This book is gorgeous – the animals are so lifelike and appealing – it makes you want to get started straight away.'
Melissa Corkhill, *The Green Parent Magazine*

128pp; 250 x 200mm; paperback; 978-1-907359-46-0

Making Simple Needle Felts

40 Inspiring Seasonal Projects
Steffi Stern

Steffi Stern brings her inimitable energy and enthusiasm to her second book, which is intended as a back-to-basics guide to making needle-felted objects. Each project includes clear instructions and photos, and Steffi also explains basic techniques that will help the reader to make many other projects by themselves.

The book contains chapters on techniques, materials, tools and accessories. There is a chapter on fairies, angels and people, and the rest of the book is organised by season; it brims with all kinds of treasures, such as pumpkins, gnomes, strawberries, baubles, birds, bees, snails, flowers, the Nativity, mice and mermaids. All the projects in the book are doable for a beginner, with some for little fingers (no needles involved), for beginners, as well as those who have more experience. Steffi's advice is, 'Have a go!'
176pp; 250 x 200mm; paperback; 978-1-907359-97-2

Ordering Books

If you have difficulties ordering Hawthorn Press books from a bookshop, you can order direct from our website **www.hawthornpress.com**, or from our UK distributor:
BookSource, 50 Cambuslang Road, Glasgow, G32 8NB
Tel: (0845) 370 0063   Email: orders@booksource.net.

Details of our overseas distributors can be found on our website.

Hawthorn Press

www.hawthornpress.com